How to Demon

Health, Money & Friends

(1924)

Gertrude Bradford

ISBN 0-7661-0555-5

Kessinger Publishing's Rare Reprints
Thousands of Scarce and Hard-to-Find Books!

- •   •   •
- •   •   •
- •   •   •
- •   •   •
- •   •   •
- •   •   •
- •   •   •
- •   •   •
- •   •   •
- •   •   •
- •   •   •
- •   •   •
- •   •   •
- •   •   •
- •   •   •
- •   •   •
- •   •   •
- •   •   •
- •   •   •

We kindly invite you to view our extensive catalog list at:
http://www.kessinger.net

How to Demonstrate Health, Money, Friends

By

Gertrude A. Bradford

*NOW is the Eternal Reality of Life. Through-
out all Eternity, NOW is the Only Opportunity
You Will Ever Have. You Are Creating SUC-
CESS or FAILURE*

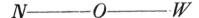

$$N\text{------}O\text{------}W$$

L. N. FOWLER & Co.
LUDGATE CIRCUS, LONDON

PUBLISHED BY
THE ELIZABETH TOWNE CO., INC.
HOLYOKE, MASS.

To my dear mother, who is with me no longer but whose love still lives in my heart, and to my two sons whose unwavering faith in my every act has been a constant inspiration when clouds hung low, and to my many friends and students whose loving interest in my work has urged me on, this book is lovingly dedicated.

—GERTRUDE A. BRADFORD.

I

The Law of Attraction; or Mental Dominion

*A*RE *you mentally alert, physically fit and morally firm? Do you know that every time you fail, right there and then, an opportunity is presented?*

Do you know that every thought which you project into the majestic sea of ether about you, adds to your success or failure?

Do you know that every thought is either attractive, selective or projective, and that you can determine what shall come into your life by a law as definite as that of mathematics?

Why continue to strive and struggle for the good things of life when you can attract them to you easily?

The law of attraction is the first thing you need to learn and apply in order to gain health, happiness and prosperity easily and quickly; and if you apply this law for the perfecting of every department of your life, you cannot fail.

The first thing you should know about this Law of Attraction is: you *can* have whatsoever you want in this life—money, power, love, friendship, health, happiness; social, political or financial position.

Take your choice or choose them all; just as you like—and get this thought so firmly fixed in your consciousness that it will become a subconscious conviction for IT IS YOUR SUBCONSCIOUS CONVICTIONS, ATTITUDES AND

HABITS THAT DETERMINE EVERY CON-
DITION IN YOUR LIFE AND ENVIRON-
MENT, AS WELL AS YOUR PHYSICAL,
MORAL AND MENTAL ATTAINMENT. To
prove this statement, start today, and every day
for one month rid your mind of some old conviction or attitude which you have been holding
toward various departments of your life, and
watch the good flow to you in rivers of peace and
joy.

Especially rid your consciousness of those convictions which have been stirring up discord in
your affairs and the affairs of relatives and
friends; those convictions due to childhood training and education.

Analyze the processes of your mental activity
in this fashion: *Has this idea I have been holding concerning my neighbor brought me any
good? Has it added to my health, happiness or
prosperity in any way? Has my prejudice against
certain styles added to my good in a material
way? Has my fear of public or private opinion
enriched myself or family? Has my antagonism
to creeds, other than my own favored one, in-
creased my circle of friends? Has my continual
reproach and unkind criticism of others made me
more beautiful or manly?* And after this analysis, if your answer is NO; then go and cleanse
your mind of these "workers of iniquity," for
until you do, you cannot "enter into the kingdom."

Every prejudice, every criticism that would
make another less than the Son of God is "that
old serpent, the devil" that will keep you out of
your Garden of Eden.

If you have been unhappy, ill, discouraged or impoverished for even one year, this is proof positive that your thinking has been largely wrong for that period of time, probably longer. Change your mental attitudes, for if they have not added to the good of yourself and family, THEY ARE WRONG, NO MATTER IF THEY ARE THE RESULT OF YOUR PARENTAL TRAINING AND EDUCATION. DON'T BE AFRAID TO GO BACK ON "YER RAISIN'" FOR ONLY SO DOES THE WORLD PROGRESS.

When you quit protesting against conditions as they are and begin to proclaim your right to "life, liberty and the pursuit of happiness," according to the dictates of your own conscience, then only will you have "dominion over all the earth," as the creator designed that you should.

This too, I want you to get firmly fixed in your subconsciousness, because you have been reasoning along just the opposite lines: No human being but yourself is to blame for one bit of your misery or unhappiness and the sooner you quit blaming others for your misfortune, the sooner your good fortune will come to you.

All depends upon your desires, your decisions, the quality of your thought, your concentration and your obedience to psychological law. When your desires and the quality of your thought correspond, that is the psychological moment. Then things begin to happen.

Man was created to have dominion over all the earth, except his fellowmen. That means YOU were created to have dominion over every

condition and circumstance in your life but
NEVER over your fellowmen. Right here is
where the majority of people make their great
mistake. They put the "cart before the horse"
by trying to gain dominion over their fellowmen
instead of over circumstances and conditions in
their life and then spend the rest of their time
wondering why they fail in everything they undertake to accomplish.

*You have no right to dictate to another, no
matter who that other may be — whether husband, wife, child, sister, brother, mother, father,
friend or business associate; and the minute you
do, you start trouble for yourself which will continue as long as you have the dictatorial attitude and until you get rid of it.*

*When no occasion can provoke you to dicta-
tion, then you may know that you have gotten
rid of it, and not until then.*

Dictation will give you temporary control of
a situation but the "cure will prove worse than
the disease." The dictatorial quality always attracts the opportunity for dictation. It always
has and always will produce trouble, and it never
produces anything else but trouble, in your life
or the life of any other human being. Therefore, the dictatorial attitude is the first mental
condition to be eliminated before any great good
can be attracted into your life.

This destructive quality is expressed in three
ways, mental, verbal and physical, and the mental dictation is the worst of the three, because,
when verbal or physical dictation is used, the
one who is subject to such dictation has the priv-

ilege of refusing to be dominated, but when the
dictation is mental, he has no chance whatever
to combat it.

In his ignorance of the Laws of Mind, he gets
antagonistic toward you; he becomes irritated
at your mere presence and begins to scheme
against you, very often becoming so extreme in
his antipathy that he attempts to injure you
without any seeming reason.   He is unable to
explain his attitude toward you but he feels your
mental vibrations of dominion and is merely trying to preserve his own mental freedom.

God never dictates to anyone but leaves every
one to do as he pleases, no matter what he pleases
to do.   He gives every man the privilege of
learning by experience; in fact, He gave us no
other way, for, while He gave us "the Law and
the Prophets," yet He left us to apply the Law
in our own way, and said distinctly, "every man
is unto himself the Way, the Truth and the Life."

Even the smallest child resents being "bossed"
for God gave no one the right to coerce another.
Within the soul of every man is the desire for
self preservation and that desire finds expression
in his mental, verbal and physical rebellion
against any interference toward his freedom to
do absolutely as he pleases.   IT IS THIS SPIRIT
THAT BREEDS INDIVIDUAL AND NATION-
AL STRIFE — ONE FACTION TRYING TO
DOMINATE AND THE OTHER FACTION
RISING IN REBELLION.

Before I came into the knowledge of this Law
and its operation I was unable to manage my
two growing boys and there was constant fric-

tion and misunderstanding between us, and yet I felt that my love was quite superior. Every attempt to gain control of them was met by stubborn resistance, defiance and cunning on their part until I despaired of ever having any influence with them again. My health also, had been destroyed and I was a physical and nervous wreck. My intense desire to better conditions, as well as my concentration and love, brought me a knowledge of Applied Psychology, and my first week of effort produced marvelous results.

In less than thirty days I had purged my system of cancer, tuberculosis, nervous prostration and heart trouble, besides regaining, to a great extent, the love and confidence of my dear boys; at the same time ridding myself of a great deal of real tragedy.

My sons are now young men and have had much worldly experience and yet there is a close comradery between us that is very comforting indeed. The following is taken from a letter which I received from one who is a total stranger to me but who was a "buddy" to my son during their service at one of the naval bases: "Should Harry be restored to duty I'll be glad for his sake for he was a good pal and deserves all the good things he is capable of getting out of this life and eternal happiness in the next."

Another letter from one who met him at the home of a mutual friend: "Harry read me bits of your letter to him. They are adorable. He is so beautifully devoted to you, I think it is wonderful. I am glad I could know him."

II

Your Divinity and Power

"Thou openest Thy hand and satisfieth the desire of every living thing."
"The Lord heareth them that call upon Him, that call upon Him in Truth."

GOD possesses three creative attributes by which He has created the universe and man. These three creative attributes are: Omnipotence, Omniscience and Omnipresence— All Power, All Seeing or All Wisdom, and Ever Present, hence it fills all space and interpenetrates every atom of creation. Every atom vibrates with that Divine Power and there is no life without it.

You have been taught that "man was created in the image and likeness of God," which means that MAN was and is endowed with the same creative attributes that God Himself possesses, only to a lesser degree. Therefore man has the power, in the present, to create whatsoever he wishes pertaining to human life.

God needs a universe for His unfoldment, while man only needs those things pertaining to his individual life. And God has endowed every human being with the same creative attributes which He possesses. That means that YOU HAVE THE POWER TO CREATE WHATSOEVER YOU WILL PERTAINING TO HUMAN LIFE; it means that YOU HAVE THE POWER TO DETERMINE WHAT YOU SHALL CREATE AND WHEN AND WHERE YOU WISH TO CREATE IT, AND IT ALSO MEANS THAT

YOU HAVE THE POWER TO CREATE
WHAT YOU WANT N—O—W.

Omnipotence belongs to the spiritual unfoldment, Omniscience belongs to the mental development, and Omnipresence belongs to the physical or material plane of vibration.   That is,
through spiritual unfoldment one gains Omnipotence; through mental development one gains
courage or faith, which, in its last analysis is
Omniscience; and through knowing the truth
about God's plan for man, one gains the power
to create in the present.

To be morally firm, one must have the courage
of one's convictions, and in order to have this
courage, one must know God's Truth about man
and his relation to the Divine Plan.   In fact—
health, happiness and prosperity IS in knowing
the Truth, for one cannot know the Truth without obtaining material power; hence, one must
be MENTALLY ALERT, PHYSICALLY FIT
AND MORALLY FIRM AT ALL TIMES AND
IN ALL PLACES.

You have also been taught that "God is Love,"
but have you ever stopped to analyze that statement? IF GOD IS LOVE THEN LOVE IS GOD
AND BEING GOD IS THE CREATIVE PRIN-
CIPLE OF THE ENTIRE UNIVERSE.

Love is the Creative Principle of all the good
in your life or the life of any one else; and anything and everything which adds to your comfort or your happiness was and is created by the
activity of this Creative Principle — Love.   "In
the beginning was the word (POWER) and the
word was with God (POWER) and the word

was God (LOVE)." Therefore, speak the word of love with power and get the results of LOVE IN ACTION, OR THE PERFECT DEMONSTRATION OF DIVINE ACTIVITY.

If God is Love, and Love is the Creative Principle of the Universe, and God has endowed man with the same creative attributes which God Himself possesses, then just the instant that YOU begin to express LOVE, TRUTH AND FAITH TOWARD EVERY CONDITION, CIRCUMSTANCE AND PERSON IN YOUR LIFE, just that instant you become Omnipotent, Omniscient and Omnipresent, for Love, Truth and Faith are Divine qualities.

On the other hand, just the instant you CEASE TO EXPRESS LOVE, TRUTH AND FAITH in your thoughts, words and deeds toward every condition, circumstance and person in your life, just that instant you lose your Divine Power. This is why the majority of people are floundering around like fish out of water, trying to succeed but meeting with utter failure in almost everything which they attempt to do, for if the average person expresses Love, Truth or Faith in his thoughts FIVE MINUTES DURING THE TWENTY-FOUR HOURS, he is doing extremely well. And yet it is impossible to attain success in any other way.

It is not your money nor your hard work that add to your health, happiness or prosperity, for if it were, then anyone who had money would be happy and healthy and anyone who worked hard would have health, happiness and prosperity. Yet we all know people who are ill and unhappy who have plenty of money and who have spent their lives at hard work without obtaining either condition.

What really brings you an abundance of everything good, is Love, Truth and Faith expressed in THOUGHT, WORD AND DEED. Omnipotence is gained through the expression of Love; Omniscience is gained through the expression of Faith, and Omnipresence is gained through the expression of Truth. Please note that I said these creative attributes are gained through the EXPRESSION OF LOVE, TRUTH AND FAITH IN THOUGHT, WORD AND DEED.

POWER IS QUALITY IN ACTIVITY AND THE MANIFESTATION OF WHAT YOU WANT IS BUT THE CRYSTALIZATION OF THESE DIVINE QUALITIES THROUGH THE INDIVIDUAL EXPRESSION OF YOUR THOUGHTS, WORDS AND DEEDS. THEREFORE, THE GREATER THE EXPRESSION, THE MORE PERFECT WILL BE YOUR DEMONSTRATION. For this reason, an unfailing method for the demonstration of any desire is a full and complete expression of Love, Truth, Faith, Gratitude and Praise. Each is a Divine quality and must result in Divine Power.

Love, being the Creative Principle of all life, must be all Good, therefore, Truth, Faith, Gratitude and Praise, are all phases of Love and partake of the Divine. By Love, I do not mean the limited sex expression existing between men and women, but that QUALITY OF MIND WHICH PROMPTS THE CONSTRUCTIVE ACTIONS

OF EVERY-DAY LIFE—THAT QUALITY
WHICH SEEKS THE GOOD OF OTHERS
WHILE SEEKING YOUR OWN GOOD, realizing that seeking for others what you seek for
yourself is the truest brotherhood that can exist.
The quicker you help others to obtain their desires, the quicker your own will be realized.

You must also understand the meaning of
TRUTH, FAITH, GRATITUDE AND PRAISE,
for it is our understanding of the great fundamentals of life which enables us to apply the
LAW scientifically and produce definite results.
Truth, as applied to life, is the understanding of
man's relation to God and his place in the Divine
Plan of Creation.   Knowing this relation, is
what frees man from the limitation of sin, disease and failure, and brings him into his divine
heritage of health, happiness and prosperity.

Man is God's perfect idea, possessing every
quality of Divine Mind and he was created to
EXPRESS these qualities.   If he works with
this Law instead of against it, everything must
work together for his good and his desires must
be made manifest, for man's desire for good is
God's desire seeking expression through the very
channel which God created for that purpose.

Because you were created to fill a definite
place in life, you were endowed with special talents and abilities, through the expression of
which you would attract the experiences best
suited to your development for this place.   Your
good desire, then, is merely your own good seeking manifestation through its proper channel,

and is God's way of breathing into your nostrils the BREATH OF LIFE.

Faith must also find active expression through the understanding, and this is not as difficult as it may seem. FAITH IS IN KNOWING, AND TO KNOW IS TO HAVE FAITH. Knowing the Truth about the relation existing between God and His perfect idea, man, is to have faith, for one cannot realize the Truth without gaining faith.

Faith, even as a grain of mustard seed, has power to remove mountains, hence your faith in the integrity of man, woman or child must meet with a response. But your faith must come from knowing that Love is Omnipotent, and that a feeling of sincere friendship expressed in thought, word and deed, must make a connection with that same quality in others, and will in turn, be expressed to you. Therefore, you have nothing to doubt or fear.

Gratitude, actively expressed, makes you a human magnet of good fortune. The thought of gratitude alone is not sufficient, for it is the QUALITY OF GRATITUDE BEING ACTIVELY EXPRESSED which attracts the good, and this, as well as all other Divine qualities, must be directed toward the source of All Good as well as to the human channel. THIS DUAL EXPRESSION IS WHAT MOST PEOPLE NEGLECT.

A perfect expression of any constructive quality is necessary for a perfect demonstration. Remember that A PERFECT EXPRESSION MEANS, IN THOUGHT, WORD AND DEED.

I often have folk tell me that they do not consider it necessary to verbally express their gratitude to human beings as long as they are grateful to God for what they get. Just as often, I have people tell me they do not consider it necessary to be grateful to God as long as they are grateful to those who have been instrumental in bringing them good, and sometimes I meet those who say they have no one to thank for their good, that it was due to their own efforts.

WE ACCOMPLISH NOTHING ALONE. And unless every good quality is made active in thought, word and deed, toward God and your fellowmen for their cooperation, there is not a full expression and your demonstration will be imperfect.

Remember that God dwells in the heart of every man, therefore, LOVE, TRUTH, FAITH, GRATITUDE AND PRAISE, cultivated in the thoughts and radiated verbally and physically toward your fellowmen, conscious at the same time that each is but a temple for the Living God, reaches the throne of Grace. That is how the Holy Command, "praise God continually,'" is made possible.

"Whoso offereth PRAISE glorifieth me; and to him that ordereth his conversation aright will I show the salvation of God."

Praise is another quality that too often fails to find activity in the life of an individual. We are prone to praise with rapturous enthusiasm a work of art, but how often do YOU, dear reader, praise those with whom you come in close contact?

Ah, so you think there is very little that is praiseworthy about your husband, your wife, your unruly son or daughter, and the neighbor who constantly annoys you with her peculiar way of doing and talking. They "are all wrong from birth," sums up your idea of them, so you avoid them as much as possible and are indifferent to everything except their imperfections. You spend no time whatever on taking note of their lovely qualities, so your eyesight becomes less keen to the beauties of life as the result of your bad habit of inverted vision, and after a time, it begins to show in the conditions of your life and in the ill health of your physical body.

Your attitude of unkind criticism always repels the good while an attitude of praise always attracts your good. Unkind criticism lies in trying to show up an error or imperfection of an individual instead of trying to reveal the Truth about him; in allowing your mind to dwell upon his faults instead of upon him as unchangeable good, or as God's perfect idea. Those who are closely associated with us always reflect our dominant virtues or our dominant vices.

I once had a student who had the habit of repelling her good through her trait of unkind criticism, and her method of applying the Law to attract her desires and overcome the habit is quite worth while repeating. She was a great lover of physical beauty and when she met a man or woman who was seemingly devoid of commendable traits of character she would study their physical body for something to praise. In one, she would praise shapely hands; in another, she would make favorable comment upon the shape and color of the eyes; in others, the well-groomed feet would attract her admiration, and the graceful carriage of others never failed to meet with her verbal approval.

I remember one night, she was having dinner at one of the well-known cafes, and her attention was attracted to a woman at one of the tables who, to all appearances, did not live the conventional life, but my young friend remarked that "her method of eating was a symphony of good breeding." Gradually this student overcame her habit of unkind criticism, until she developed one of the most fascinating personalities that I know.

Good must always return to us from any source to which we direct Love, Truth, Faith, Gratitude and Praise, and evil will always return to us from any source to which we direct evil. Sincerity begets sincerity and insincerity begets insincerity. Constructive qualities, however, must be held toward people in general as well as to people in particular, and every prejudice, hatred and unkind criticism, only prevents your desires from becoming manifested.

WE ALWAYS OBTAIN OUR DESIRES BY HELPING OTHERS TO OBTAIN THEIR DESIRES AND THE MORE WE AID OTHERS TO OBTAIN, THE MORE AND GREATER WILL BE OUR MANIFESTATIONS.

III

How Your Mind Creates

"I will declare the decree: the Lord hath said unto me,
THOU ART MY SON; THIS DAY have I begotten thee."

NO doubt you have heard of Aladdin and his Magic Lamp. If YOU had this magic lamp, right this minute, what would you choose in the way of environment and achievement?

You have the same power that Aladdin had to create what you want in your life now — here and now — only instead of rubbing a lamp, you merely put into operation the hidden forces of your mind. You arouse into constructive activity every department of your sub-conscious and super-conscious being and your life is never the same again, but grows and develops according to your vision and the quality of your thought.

There is one fundamental law by which man in general and YOU IN PARTICULAR, determine the nature of every manifestation in your life, and it is your conscious or unconscious obedience to this law which determines every condition, circumstance and creation of every individual development. That law is: WHATSOEVER THE MIND DWELLS UPON MUST BECOME MANIFEST IN THE LIFE IN SOME CONDITION OF GOOD OR EVIL, ACCORDING TO THE QUALITY OF THE THOUGHT. This law is called THE LAW OF ATTRACTION.

Every thought you think creates something in your life — romance, deadly monotony, enemies, friends, discord, harmony, poverty, opulence, tragedy, sickness, health, or happiness — all is created by the control and quality of your thoughts.

NOTHING CAN COME BACK TO YOU UNTIL IT FIRST GOES OUT FROM YOUR MIND. EVERY THOUGHT YOU SEND OUT RETURNS TO YOU A FREIGHT OF JOY OR SORROW, ACCORDING TO THE QUALITY OF THE INITIAL IMPULSE.

NO MAN ESCAPES THE CONSEQUENCES OF HIS OWN THINKING, ALTHOUGH HE MAY ESCAPE THE CONSEQUENCES OF HIS ACTIONS; FOR MANY PEOPLE ACT DIFFERENTLY THAN THEY THINK. That Law is absolute and is called the Law of Compensation, or the Law of Divine Justice, and applies to king and peasant, rich and poor, alike.

You are exactly like a wireless telegraph instrument and your mental vibrations connect you with other magnetic centers of Mind who are attuned to your quality of consciousness. You are a human magnet, or a magnetic center of Mind, for the entire universe is governed and created by Mind — God's Mind and man's mind.

GOD'S MIND CREATES EVERYTHING PERTAINING TO THE UNIVERSAL LIFE AND MAN'S MIND CREATES EVERYTHING PERTAINING TO HUMAN LIFE. It is gross ignorance of this fact that has prevented man from demonstrating the words of Jesus Christ to the effect: "believe on me and the works that I do ye shall do also and even greater works than these."

Man is a co-worker with God, despite the fact that he has failed to realize this before and since the time of Jesus. Many people have asked me if I believe the whole Bible, and I say, YES, and if YOU DO then you MUST BELIEVE THE PROMISES OF JESUS AND OTHER DIVINE PROMISES CONTAINED IN THE BIBLE.

By every morsel of food you eat, and by every drop of nourishing liquid that you drink, and by every bit of air that you breathe, you generate an electricity that is the most powerful force in the universe, outside of the God Force which envelops all, fills all space and permeates everything with Its everlasting life.

This God Force is a sea of magnetic ether and you are always in touch with it, for it interpenetrates your body and holds it together. You have this marvelous power always at your command and you use it every minute of your life, although you do not use it as much as you should, or you would be a genius as the world understands its meaning. Everybody breathes in this wonder-working energy in the same way but expresses it differently, and IT IS IN THE METHOD OF EXPRESSION THAT SUFFERING OR HAPPINESS IS ATTRACTED.

Each expression of a thought brings forth coin marked by the stamp of evil or good, according to the quality of the initial impulse. AS YOU EXPRESS A QUALITY, A CONVICTION OR AN ATTITUDE, IT BECOMES CRYSTALIZED POWER AND TAKES TANGIBLE FORM, BECOMING A CONDITION, CIRCUMSTANCE, OR PHYSICAL MANIFESTATION.

Why not make every condition in your life crystalized Love, Truth, Faith, Gratitude, or Praise?   You can always determine just how much of the Divine qualities you are expressing by the amount and quality of good which you are ATTRACTING.

Those who attract the most loving service are those whose hearts throb with the longing to serve humanity as a whole by serving those nearest at hand regardless of creed, color or nation.   They are those whose souls see in everything the reflection of the Christ and serve as unto God (Love), expressing continually the Divine qualities toward all — excluding none, including each and every one.

Prof. Tyndall said: "The same power that forms the tear-drop, molds the planet — expression does it."   Judge Leighten Allan says: "Thoughts become molds into which Divine Energy flows, thus do we make our thoughts concrete outer forms."   If our lives are misery in all its different manifestations, we should be appalled that our thoughts are of like character, and set about to remedy the condition by a mental house-cleaning.

We should make our thought-molds turn out models of beauty — health, power, happiness and success, and cease the criminal habit of adding our product of wrong thinking to the burden of the world.

Demonstration is natural, not magical; it all comes through the expression of the Divine qualities.   Every time you express one of the Divine qualities mentally, you are making a demonstration of good, and every time you eliminate a destructive attitude of mind, you are demonstrating good.

Every time you express a thought of dictation, hate, fear, anger, or worry, you are giving more life and power to the Devil (evil). You are setting imps of Satan about the Devil's business, and because of the law of Reciprocity, they turn about and work for you as you did for them, bringing you offerings of trouble and worry.

Every time you express an evil thought, you advertise the Devil's business and it pays you for the advertising you have done in untold misery. Through the expression of hate, fear, anger, worry, and all other destructive emotions, we connect ourselves with people of like vibration and these people, being destructive, help to drag us down.

Our salvation lies in connecting ourselves with the power for good in the universe. This is done through connecting mentally with powerful people, and we can only make this connection by expressing the Divine qualities.

Every expression of nobility connects us with those pitched to the same degree of nobility, so it is important to cultivate and declare these qualities by word and deed, that we may connect with the highest channels of wisdom and genius, as well as with the great Over-soul of creation. This attracts to us those who will help us to achieve.

If you are all the time meeting those who oppose you and your desires, CHANGE — strive to

be more indulgent toward those less fortunate
than yourself, more patient toward those who do
not know the Law as well as you do, more char-
itable toward those who seemingly transgress
the Law wilfully and ignorantly, and opposing
forces will scatter, for the relationship you have
established with great minds and the Cosmic
Consciousness at once lifts you out of your environment and places you in another much more
to your liking, and one which will bring you further advancement.

Like Aladdin, everything you undertake will
prosper — you have but to rub the lamp of your
inner consciousness and your mental forces will
obey your slightest command. DESIRE IS SUC-
CESS SEEKING CRYSTALIZATION INTO
OUTER FORM THROUGH YOUR TALENTS
AND ABILITIES. THEREFORE THERE IS
A WAY TO EXPRESS IT. SEEK THE WAY
AND YOU WILL BE GIVEN THE LIGHT TO
FIND IT. THUS THE LAW OF OMNI-
SCIENCE WILL BECOME OPERATIVE
THROUGH YOU.

EVERY HUMAN BEING IS ENDOWED
WITH THE SAME CREATIVE ATTRIBUTES
WHICH GOD POSSESSES, ONLY TO A LES-
SER DEGREE. THESE ATTRIBUTES, OP-
ERATING THROUGH YOU, GIVE YOU THE
POWER TO CREATE ANY CONDITION YOU
MAY DESIRE; THE POWER TO DETER-
MINE WHAT THAT CONDITION SHALL BE,
AND THE POWER TO CREATE THAT CON-
DITION NOW.

IV

Mental Destructive Qualities

AS there are five constructive qualities which make you a magnet of good, so there are five destructive qualities which make you a magnet of ill fortune. *These five qualities of thought produce Insanity, Tragedy, Murder, Suicide, and Chronic Illness in human life. If these five mental states did not exist in human consciousness, these five conditions could not exist in human experience.*

HATE, FEAR, ANGER, WORRY, AND UNKIND CRITICISM, ARE THE FIVE ENEMIES OF YOUR EXISTENCE, AND THE ONLY REAL ENEMIES WHICH YOU POSSESS. Every one of these will attract evil and repel the good, and the only way to prevent trouble from manifesting is to get rid of these five destructive traits of character.

Like the wireless telegraph, your thought connects you with every one on earth who is pitched to your same degree of mental vibration. Every time you are angry you make a mental connection with other centers of consciousness who vibrate to that same degree of anger; every time you experience hate, fear, worry, unkind criticism, or any other destructive emotion, you attach yourself to every human being pitched to the same degree of emotion with yourself, and you do this because THOUGHT IS INSTANTANEOUS AND UNIVERSAL. It travels faster than heat or light, and light travels about 186,-

000 miles per second, so you see what a wonderful power you continually have at your command.

In addition to attaching yourself to other magnetic centers who are in tune with your vibrations, whenever you express hate, fear, etc., you add to the quantity and quality of the emotion in every heart with which you have made a mental connection, thereby attracting into your life people who criticize you, those who are dishonest and unjust to you and those who often try to injure you.

NEVER, AS LONG AS YOU LIVE, CAN YOU RID YOUR LIFE OF DISAGREEABLE PEOPLE, AS LONG AS YOU HAVE THE QUALITIES OF CONSCIOUSNESS WHICH ATTRACT THEM. ELIMINATE THE DESTRUCTIVE STATES OF THOUGHT AND YOU WILL NO LONGER HAVE YOUR LIFE MADE MISERABLE BY OFFENSIVE, OBNOXIOUS AND DISGUSTING PERSONS WHO SEEMINGLY LIVE TO ANNOY YOU AND WHO ALWAYS MISUNDERSTAND YOU.

Eliminate entirely any one of these destructive emotions from the consciousness and you will cease to attract those who have that particular emotion as a dominant mental trait, or at least those who will express that trait toward you. Wholly purge the quality of jealousy from your consciousness and you will no longer attract jealous people; eliminate the quality of anger, which means impatience, irritability and nervousness, and you will no longer attract those whose dominant trait is anger.

ELIMINATION MEANS ELIMINATION, AND NOT REPRESSION. TRUE SELF-CONTROL IS THOUGHT CONTROL AND NOT MERELY THE CONTROL OF THE PHYSICAL BODY OR ITS ACTIONS. REPRESSION IS NEVER ELIMINATION, NOR IS IT CONTROL.

According to the great fundamental Law of Creation, whatsoever the mind dwells upon must become manifest in the life in some condition of good or evil, according to the quality of the thought. And right here I want to say, that *quality of thought means the emotion with which a thought is sent forth from the mind. Every time your mind dwells upon the faults of another human being, you help hypnotize that person into continuing his fault, you intensify that very condition you criticize and are trying to eliminate, and you make that very fault manifest in your life through your own habits and through those with whom you are the most closely associated — husband, wife, children, sisters, brothers, father, mother, friends, and business colleagues.*

It is only in this way that the Law of Compensation can mete out absolute justice individually and collectively, and it is so that we suffer or are made happy according to the thoughts which we send out to the world in general and to individuals in particular, making or marring our own lives as we make or mar the lives of others by our thinking.

There is one thought which, if held scientifically and with its scientific interpretation, will free any man, woman or child from the negative hypnotic influences and cause them to radiate the ideal qualities toward anyone holding this thought for their benefit. The thought which follows must be held with a feeling of sincere friendship: "WHAT GOD HATH JOINED TO-GETHER," NO POWER CAN PUT ASUNDER. What God hath joined together, which is man and his ideal, or man and GOD'S PERFECT IDEA OF MAN, no power can put asunder.

God and His perfect idea are inseparable and as His perfect idea of man is man's ideal, no one has any desire to desecrate that ideal unless under the hypnotic influence of evil. The reason why the majority of people are not expressing their ideals is because they are controlled by the perverted vision of evil, but the ideal is there just the same and must find expression in the life as soon as they are freed from the evil power which has mastered them.

Freedom from the bondage of wrong doing is the only impelling force needed for immediate regeneration of mental and spiritual faculties and this regeneration will take place as soon as this scientific thought is held with a feeling of SIN-CERE FRIENDSHIP, although it may not be openly acknowledged.

Some people are very slow to acknowledge openly a change of heart and very often refuse to do so until the regeneration is complete. Remember that LOVE IS OMNIPOTENT AND NO CONDITION, CIRCUMSTANCE OR PER-SON CAN RESIST THAT FORCE. IT IS AL-SO A DIVINE TRUTH THAT "LOVE IS THE

FULFILLING OF THE LAW;" HENCE, SOON
OR LATE, THROUGH SUFFERING AND
SICKNESS, ONE MUST LEARN TO LOVE
THAT WHICH HAS BEEN HATED.   THE
DECREE IS DIVINE, THEREFORE "EVERY
KNEE SHALL BOW."

The next step to be considered in getting defin-
ite results is the analysis of sincere friendship.
What is SINCERE FRIENDSHIP? STOP AND
THINK WHAT IT MEANS TO YOU AND YOU
WILL BETTER REALIZE JUST WHAT IT
MEANS TO ANOTHER.

Whenever you have a friend whom you consider sincere, it is because he is a friend to you
in spite of your faults.   He utterly ignores your
pettiness and even takes pleasure in being indulgent toward you whenever your actions are
criticised by others.   NOT ONLY IS YOUR
FRIEND INDULGENT, BUT HE TAKES
YOUR PART AND DOES EVERYTHING
WITHIN HIS POWER TO SHIELD YOU
FROM UNKIND CRITICISM.

THIS IS THE SORT OF FRIENDSHIP YOU
MUST CULTIVATE IN YOUR HEART FOR
OTHERS IF YOU DESIRE SUCCESS TO BE
A PERMANENT CONDITION IN YOUR LIFE.
Not for one or two only must this attitude be
cultivated, but toward ALL, regardless of what
they may have done to injure you.

If you put one person out of your life BE-
CAUSE OF HIS FAULTS, you do not know
what sincere friendship is, nor have you cultivated that quality in your heart.   "TO EXCLUDE
ONE IS TO EXCLUDE ALL AND TO EX-

CLUDE ALL IS TO EXCLUDE THE ONE."
Remember this bit of ancient wisdom when you
lose, through gossip, indifference or criticism,
those who are near and dear to you.

The Bible says, "HE THAT HATETH HIS
BROTHER IS A MURDERER."   This does
not mean a brother in the personal sense, for
"God is no respecter of persons;" and JESUS
said, "Who is my mother? and who are my breth-
ren?" Any human being is your brother or sister, according to the words of Jesus.

Suspicion of others, jealousy, envy and unkind
criticism in your thoughts will cause these same
qualitites to be expressed toward you through
those who are nearest and dearest. THE VERY
SUREST   WAY   TO   DIRECT   SUSPICION
TOWARD YOURSELF IS TO DIRECT   IT
TOWARD SOMEONE ELSE.   REMEMBER
THAT YOUR SUSPICION OF A BROTHER IS
JUST AS GROUNDLESS AS HIS SUSPICION
OF YOU, FOR SUSPICION IS NOT A GOD
QUALITY. What if he is doing something fool-
ish or unbrotherly, YOUR NOTICE of it only
directs it to yourself and your loved ones.

THE CHRONIC INVALID IS THAT PER-
SON WHO, BY WRONG THINKING GEN-
ERATES POISON IN THE BLOOD FASTER
THAN THE MEDICINE OF THE DOCTOR
OR THE NATURAL FUNCTIONS OF THE
BODY CAN PURGE IT OUT. You can readily
see that this Truth puts more people in the
chronic class than are recognized as such, because
those that take, first one disease and then an-
other are just as surely chronic invalids as are

those who just continue to manifest one form of disease. In fact, the latter have a greater chance for recovery than the former, for a continued form of one disease denotes that there is but one mental condition to change, while in the other cases almost the entire consciousness is destructive and there are MANY mental changes to be wrought.

For this very reason a metaphysician very often finds it an easy task to cure a chronic invalid after the medical specialists have failed. The metaphysician first of all teaches the patient the Truth about the action of Mind: Spiritual Cause, material effect, and then teaches that spiritual harmony alone will produce harmony in the body and life. If the one being treated is sufficiently interested in obtaining health, happiness and prosperity, he will at once comply with the instructions and cleanse his thoughts of the death-producing qualities, and there is only one result — PERFECT HEALTH.

By allowing the mind to dwell upon an imperfect condition of any kind, a corresponding emotion is thereby created and this emotion re-acts upon your body as physical suffering and upon your life as discord. In this way you punish yourself for every wrong thing which you have thought and God is in no way responsible for your trials and tribulations.

God has given you the power and the privilege of creating whatsoever you desire, and He has given you the Law by which to determine what your creations shall be, and if through your ignorance or poor understanding, you misapply the Law, you have no one but yourself to blame for the result.

God and all the God forces of the universe stand ready to cooperate with you the minute you apply the Law correctly. NO LONGER BLAME GOD FOR YOUR SUFFERING AND INSIST THAT IT IS GOD'S WILL, FOR YOU UTTER A FALSEHOOD EVERY TIME YOU DO SO. OUR SUFFERING IS FOR OUR SALVATION, IN THAT IT SHOULD AWAKEN US TO THE FACT THAT WE ARE GETTING AWAY FROM GOD'S LAW. WHEN YOU ARE SICK, POOR AND UNHAPPY, THERE IS SOMETHING WRONG WITH YOUR MENTAL PROCESSES.

The universe is governed by an Infinite Law of Justice, and this Law of Justice makes it imperative that man shall create and become either master or slave of his creations. Every creation is attached to its creator and must affect his life just as he intends it to affect the lives of others, thus man creates his own punishment and his own reward and so becomes a free agent to work in connection with the Law of God (good) or against it. To work against it, trouble and suffering is the one and only result.

Every attitude, conviction and thought must create some condition, circumstance or effect in the life of an individual. NONE ESCAPE. ALL MUST PAY TO THE UTTERMOST FARTHING. THE LAW DOES NOT EQUIVOCATE NOR SHOW PARTIALITY TO ANY RACE, CREED OR PERSON. So, when you hold a thought of hate, anger or unkind criticism

toward anyone because of something he has done
and then watch for a return of the offense, you
hypnotize him into doing the very thing for
which you condemned him, and no one but yourself is to blame for the result.

Your strong, clear picture of him, committing
an act of injustice or dishonesty is magnetic and
will in time come into manifestation, even though
you hold it without any particular emotion. But
a watchful attitude, coupled with an intense emotion of hate, fear, anger, worry or unkind criticism, will sometimes produce immediate results
and always meets with an instant response,
though it does not always become evident at once.
Every one of these destructive thoughts attract
discordant conditions in the life of an individual,
just as thoughts of Love, Truth, Faith, Gratitude and Praise attract health, happiness and
prosperity.

Thoughts of unkind criticism, anger, irritability and opposition, are all phases of hate and
must always attract discord. You, being their
creator, must reap what you have sown. The effect of any destructive attitude often returns to
the operator from unexpected sources and the cry
goes forth, "Why, I have never injured that
man!" But the Law is inexorable and is presented in its various forms and phases that man
may learn the great lesson of THOUGHT-CON-
TROL; to first learn to control himself and thereby control his destiny.

By reversing your old habits of thought into
constructive channels, you will also attract the
good from unexpected sources and in unexpected

ways, for a new way of thinking must create new conditions and circumstances in your life and attract to you those who will cooperate with you in establishing the new and desired order of things.

To avoid the old mental actions and reactions, and to create new mental habits and qualities, try memorizing daily ten constructive words, with their definitions and proper pronunciations; also memorize a constructive bit of poetry or prose. Just a little thought by Service may give you a new idea:

> "Sometimes I wonder, after all,
>   Amid this tangled web of Fate,
> If what is great may not be small,
>   And what is small may not be great.
> So wondering, I go my way,
>   Yet in my heart contentment sings.
> O may I ever see, I pray,
>   God's grace and love in Little Things."

Kipling's "IF," for your rule of conduct in acquiring complete mastery may also be good mental discipline:

> "If you can keep your head when all about you
> Are losing theirs and blaming it on you;
> If you can trust yourself when all men doubt you
> And make allowance for their doubting, too;
> If you can wait and not be tired by waiting,
> Or being lied about, don't deal in lies,
> Or being hated, don't give way to hating,
> And yet don't look too good nor talk too wise;

If you can dream — and not make dreams your
    master;
If you can think and not make thoughts your
    aim;
If you can meet with Triumph and Disaster
And treat those two imposters just the same;
If you can bear to hear the truth you've spoken
Twisted by knaves to make a trap for fools,

Or watch the things you gave your life to,
    broken,
And stoop and build 'em up with worn-out tools;
If you can make one heap of all your winnings
And risk it on one turn of pitch and toss
And lose, and start again at your beginnings
And never breathe a word about your loss;
If you can force your nerve and heart and sinew
To serve their turn long after they are gone,
And so hold on when there is nothing in you
Except the Will which says to them, 'Hold on!'

If you can talk with crowds and keep your vir-
    tue,
Or walk with Kings — nor lose the common
    touch,
If neither foes nor loving friends can hurt you,
If all men count with you but none too much;
If you can fill the unforgiving minute
With sixty seconds' worth of distance run,
Yours is the Earth, and everything that's in it,
And, — which is more — you'll be a man, my
    son!"

V

Triune Man
Conscious, Subconscious, Super-
conscious

OUT of the Soul of the Universe a man is formed. Out of the Cosmic Ether appears his guiding star—his inspiration and his desires, which, if followed, develop his physical body, unfold his abilities and reveal his talents, leading him to final achievement and his coveted goal.

Attracted by the mental vision ever before him — his vision of ultimate attainment — and impelled forward by the constructive energy which is being constantly generated within him, through his expression of the Divine Qualities, there can be only one result —SUCCESS.

Man has three minds, conscious, subconscious and superconscious; each has a distinct function to perform and neither should be allowed to infringe or usurp the duties of the other, for only misfortune occurs whenever this is done.

THE CONSCIOUS MIND IS THE MIND OF THE FIVE SENSES, IT DEALS ONLY WITH EXTERNALS AND ALWAYS REASONS FROM WITHOUT. It judges by appearances and expresses every destructive thought. It determines what shall be the nature of your creations and makes the mental blueprint by which your subconscious mind builds into your life conditions according to your mental pictures and the quality of your consciousness.

It is your conscious mind which goes to sleep, or faints whenever you experience some strong emotion. It is your conscious mind that succumbs to the influence of an anæsthetic, or which ceases to function when you are in a trance.

The Subconscious Mind is the seat of memory and habit. It contains every impression and suggestion that has ever been given by you or to you since the day you were conceived in your mother's womb. It is also your good or bad servant, which builds into your life and into your body the result of every thought you think, according to its quality. It builds into your life and into your body the effects of your dominant mental attitudes and convictions.

By your thinking you direct and control the subconscious to do your bidding. It is always directed and controlled by suggestion, which must be given mentally, verbally, physically, or veiled, and it always builds into your life first, those suggestions which are expressed the most and *expressed with the strongest emotion.*

Those suggestions which arrest the undivided attention of the subconscious mind always arouse its determination for expressing those suggestions, for it is a psychological law that THE DETERMINATION OF THE SUBCONSCIOUS MIND ALWAYS LIES AT ONE'S POINT OF INTEREST. Therefore if you want an outward manifestation, always be interested in making the same condition manifest in the lives of others for in this way you put into operation the Law of Manifestation, which will react in your life, as well as in the lives of others.

The prenatal attitudes and convictions of the mother, transmitted to the subconscious mind of her child, is what constitutes heredity. If the child, whether or not he understands the science of the mind, transmits this same mental state on to the next generation of children, he has intensified it by allowing his mind to dwell upon it and by expressing it mentally, verbally and physically. In this way a thought gathers both energy and momentum, until it becomes a deed of greatness or of crime, according to the initial impulse which sent it forth.

Not so long ago I had occasion to analyze a case which illustrates the action of the subconscious mind in making manifest in the child the prenatal attitude of the mother.

This woman to whom I refer had, in her early life become enamored of a man who betrayed her trust. Her seeming love for the father of her unborn child, turned to bitter hatred and she planned many times to kill him for his perfidy, which forced her to face motherhood and the censure of society, alone and unprotected.

Each resolution she made to take his life failed to be carried out, but she nursed the thought of hatred in her heart for many years. However, she married, moved to another locality and lived the life of the average married woman.

When her son reached the age of twenty-two years he became enamored of a young woman who refused to become the mother of his child, and in a moment of uncontrolled prenatal hatred he shot and killed her.

Court testimony proved that the slain woman

had refused to become the mother of his child by resorting to the unholy act of an illegal operation. The murder emotion in her own heart became the attracting force for the prenatal thought of murder held in his own subconscious mind, which precipitated or crystalized the mental quality into outer or material form. The subconscious mind of the boy had been seeking an activating motive for making manifest the mental blueprint of the prenatal emotion of murder placed there by the mother years before.

The subconscious mind never sleeps and is just as busy when you are asleep as when you are awake. In fact, it is more sentient during your period of rest than when your daily round of domestic and business duties demand its attention and interest for the manifestation of immediate needs. It builds into your body and life the dominant vibrations or suggestions which it receives from the sources of good or evil with which you were *en rapport* before you put your conscious mind to sleep.

If you have gone to sleep in an angry mood or with bitter hatred in your heart, you magnetize your subconscious mind with destructive vibrations, and while you are asleep it draws to you negative vibrations from other centers of mind.

Many people awaken in the morning with a grouch, and it has been said by authorities on criminal psychology that most of the crimes are planned before ten o'clock in the morning, due to this operation of mental vibrations. YOU CAN, HOWEVER, MAKE YOUR SUBCONSCIOUS MIND ATTRACT HEALTH, HAPPI-

NESS AND PROSPERITY DURING YOUR PERIOD OF REST, AND SO REVOLUTIONIZE YOUR PHYSICAL CONDITION AS WELL AS YOUR ENVIRONMENT, BY THIS PROCESS OF PROPERLY DIRECTING THE SUBCONSCIOUS FACULTIES BEFORE YOU GO TO SLEEP.

The Superconscious Mind is the Mind of All Power, All Life, All Peace, All Happiness, and All Prosperity; it is Omnipotent, Omniscient and Omnipresent, and builds only good into your affairs. Whenever your Superconscious Mind is in control, perfect harmony of life and body is the natural result. Peace, power and plenty, in every department of your life, follows the activity of the Superconscious Mind.

SO YOU CAN SEE HOW IMPORTANT IT IS NEVER TO EXPRESS IN THOUGHT, WORD OR DEED, ANY OF THE DESTRUCTIVE EMOTIONS, AND TO THINK ONLY THOUGHTS WHICH EXPRESS THE EMOTIONS OF LOVE, TRUTH, FAITH, GRATITUDE AND PRAISE TOWARD EVERY CONDITION, EVERY CIRCUMSTANCE AND EVERY PERSON IN YOUR LIFE.

By expressing these Divine qualities of Mind, you put your Superconscious Mind in control and create a safety zone about you which absolutely protects you from the evil thoughts of others, and at the same time attracts into your life conditions and circumstances conducive to your happiness and well-being. THE SUPERCONSCIOUS MIND ALWAYS ATTRACTS PERFECTION, BECAUSE IT IS PERFECTION.

One never attracts disease when the Superconscious Mind is in control, nor can disagreeable
people become hindering factors in your environment.   Harmony in the life is in exact proportion
to the control of the Superconscious Mind.

In the Universal Plan, a place was created for
every human being that perfection should result
and individual progress be without friction and
just as long as each individual remains in his
place harmony obtains, providing the Great Law
is obeyed in other respects.   Displacement is the
result of discord as a first cause, which in turn
produces discord.   However, neither displacement nor discord can abide for any length of
time, if the thoughts are controlled by the Love
quality of consciousness, for LOVE WILL AD-
JUST EVERY SITUATION.

Because God's plan for the universe was and is
perfection, every human being was and is created
in his proper place and the material for his further advancement placed within his reach.   It is
imperative for man to reach out for the good
which lies ever before him, for in the reaching
out process, he develops the power which carries
him on to achievement.

A constant reaching out for the bigger and
better things of life results in soul growth, the
ultimate of which is SUCCESS ALONG THE
CHOSEN LINE OF VISION.   IT IS THROUGH
THE SOUL GROWTH THAT WE ACHIEVE
AND SO SUCCESS BECOMES THE ULTI-
MATE OF A SERIES OF IMPROVEMENTS,
MENTAL, MORAL AND PHYSICAL.

Neither environment, climate, nor inherited

tendencies, can prevent your final success so long as you keep your eye single and your heart pure, ever working toward a vision of attainment. Keeping the vision clear means keeping the eye single and this is a most valuable asset in obtaining your desires.   A clear vision and a pure heart crystalizes into Divine, Omnipotent Power, which will in turn, transmute every obstacle into a stepping stone and make of every enemy a friend.

IT IS THE COMMON LOT OF ALL TO MAKE ENEMIES. THE SUCCESSFUL MAN OR WOMAN BECOMES SO BY VIRTUE OF TRANSMUTING EACH ENEMY INTO A FRIEND; THE MEDIOCRE MAN OR WOMAN REMAINS SO BECAUSE THEY NOT ONLY MAKE ENEMIES, BUT KEEP THEM AS SUCH. Endeavor to be lovingly interested in every human being you meet and strive to awaken their sincere interest in you, always keeping in mind that this mutual interest will eventually result in furthering your business, social and domestic success. GET THE HABIT OF MAKING ONE NEW FRIEND EACH DAY AND PUTTING FORTH A SINCERE EFFORT TO BIND AN OLD ONE CLOSER TO YOU. HOWEVER, YOU CANNOT DO THIS BY GOSSIP, CRITICISM, OR PASSING DEROGATORY REMARKS ABOUT ANYONE.

With the aid of your conscious, subconscious and superconscious minds, and the application of Divine Law, you express Omnipotence, Omniscience and Omnipresence, as related to your individual life or destiny.

It is only through CONSTANT EXPRESSION
THAT YOU DEVELOP, UNFOLD AND
ACHIEVE SUCCESS IN YOUR CHOSEN
FIELD OF ENDEAVOR. EXPRESSION IS
DIVINE AND MAN FROM BIRTH FEELS
THE COSMIC URGE TO EXPRESS HIMSELF
AND HE DOES THIS THROUGH IMITATION,
COMPARISON AND IMPULSION.

REPRESSION IS ALWAYS A HINDRANCE
TO HEALTH, HAPPINESS AND PROSPERI-
TY BECAUSE REPRESSION IS IN DIRECT
OPPOSITION TO GOD'S LAW OF UNFOLD-
MENT, WHICH IS CONSTANT EXPRESSION.
Please realize also that repression is not control.
Control is never repression, but scientific expres-
sion. Control and repression are entirely different
in meaning, for repression is only PHYSICAL
ACTION SUBDUED, WHILE REAL SELF-
CONTROL LIES IN CONSCIOUSLY DIRECT-
ING AND FOCUSING THE THOUGHTS UPON
CONSTRUCTIVE ISSUES, REGARDLESS OF
CONDITIONS, CIRCUMSTANCES OR PER-
SONS. REPRESSION ATTRACTS THOSE
WHO WILL DOMINATE YOU AND PRE-
VENT YOUR DEVELOPMENT ALONG LINES
WHICH YOU LOVE.

IMITATION is one of the first states of consciousness acquired by an individual and this acquired trait often becomes a DOMINANT subconscious state until one finally becomes a follower
of those whose originality and individuality have
not become atrophied through disuse and the mis-
use of imitation.

We all are, more or less, creatures of imitation

and in so far as it promotes our health, happiness
and prosperity, it is good and beneficial but when
it keeps us in the mediocre class of workers it is
detrimental.

YOU WERE CREATED TO BE A LEADER
IN YOUR CHOSEN CALLING AND IF YOU
REFUSE TO FOLLOW THE DIVINE PLAN
FOR YOUR UNFOLDMENT, YOU MUST EX-
PECT TO BE A FAILURE, FOR THERE CAN
BE NO PERMANENT SUCCESS UNLESS
YOU WORK WITH THE GREAT LAW IN-
STEAD OF AGAINST IT.

IMITATION AS A DOMINANT SUBCON-
SCIOUS STATE, ALWAYS ATTRACTS FAIL-
URE. The world has no respect for one who attempts to gain success by imitation. Endeavor
to make each act of your life as well as your
speech radiate the Cosmic Consciousness which
is seeking expression through you in a way which
will make you a coin of the Realm of Infinite Wisdom.

COMPARISON, too, should be used as an aid
to the fullest unfoldment of life, individual or
collective. It is often by comparing one plan
with another that much imperfection is eliminated and it is by comparing your present development with what you hope to attain that causes
you to put forth greater effort to accomplish that
which you desire, hence comparison may be beneficial. When you compare the faults or attain-
ments of another with what YOU have accomplished in development to his detriment, then
comparison is harmful and attracts to you the
disapproval of others.

IMPULSION has to do with the Law of Periodicity, which determines the fixity of habits, whether pre-natal or acquired. Many people are mental and physical slaves to habits of disease and environment which become a part of their subconscious life through some intense parental mental impulse or desire.

Through ignorance of the Great Law, the impulse is given fresh impetus whenever the mind is allowed to dwell upon it and it goes forth as original and individual desire. It gains momentum and strength very often through repressing the physical manifestation while brooding upon it mentally, holding a vivid mental picture of it in its various phases and attracting the like vibrations of other people keyed to the same quality of vibration, and finally sending the impulse forth in a burst of uncontrollable emotion which is overpowering in its intensity and which scatters disease and sorrow broadcast as it permeates the ether and impinges upon the minds of those who are *en rapport*.

To overcome a prenatal tendency that is harmful, cease to brood upon it as the bane of your existence; cease to feel that you are inferior and deserve the scorn of society because of it. Instead, take your stand as an individual free and equal with any other and "entitled to life, liberty and the pursuit of happiness," according to the dictates of your own conscience. Seek out your talents and abilities and express your good ideas to those about you. But if you have little opportunity to express your ideas to others, then get pencil and paper and express them in writing, but express them somehow.

Decide on what you would like to accomplish in life. Get all the information you can on the subject. Ask questions about it, for those about you may have valuable information at hand which they will be more than glad to pass on to you. Get books on the subject. If you cannot buy books, borrow them from the local library or from individuals. In this way you will give new suggestions to your subconscious mind which will in time occupy so much of your time and attention that the old harmful ideas will be forgotten and be eliminated through disuse.

When old ideas and impulses control you and prove themselves harmful, get new ones of an opposite nature and *express them.* Give power to them by acting them out, remembering that IDEAS EXPRESSED IN WORD AND ACT CRYSTALIZE INTO OMNIPOTENT POWER. Memorize ten constructive words every day and learn to give them the fullest possible definition. Visualize what these words and ideas would actually mean to you were they incorporated into your daily life and habits, then try to express them as fully as possible in speech and conduct.

OPPOSITION is another mental quality that is acquired very early in life, becoming a subconscious function before the child is one year of age. This tendency, which manifests so early and which soon develops into a fixed state of consciousness, is due to the example of opposition which is a dominant mental trait of the adult mentalities with which the child is surrounded.

Meeting with opposition at the start, he very naturally opposes in return, his first opposition acting as the initial impulse of an accumulative consciousness, hence attracting experiences which react upon his physical body, determining a portion of its texture, form and personality. Each portion of the body, therefore, is the effect of an accumulated consciousness.

A woman came to me some time ago with her little boy of two years, who was wrecking her nerves with his incessant "NO," in response to everything that was said to him. When he cried, "NO" was screamed at the top of his voice, over and over again, until he went into a rage so exhausting that finally he would sob himself to sleep, constantly reiterating the one word, "NO." He was also very sullen and fought for everything he wanted.

Although both father and mother were very bright people and likeable in every way, and accomplished above the average, yet the subconscious mind of each was negative to a marked degree. After a short psycho-analysis, I requested that both she and her husband cultivate the agreeable habit toward everything, regardless of what it might be, for just one week and watch the effect on the child. Before the week was over one very rarely heard the word "NO" pass the lips of the child. The effect was so marvelous and noticeable that both parents tried to hold a more agreeable attitude in every word and deed, striving to eliminate the negative convictions from their subconscious minds, realizing that seeing a good reason in the acts and words of others meant harmony in their own lives, while taking the negative view on every issue only meant a crystalization of that quality within themselves.

As the various experiences of an individual react upon his body and life his interest is awakened, his determination focuses the attention of his subconscious mind and his reasoning or conscious mind is given birth through the basic impulse of self-preservation, which is in itself subconscious, the subconscious mind realizing that it must be controlled and directed consciously by the individual for whom it was created.

IT IS A PSYCHOLOGICAL TRUTH THAT MAN'S DETERMINATION ALWAYS LIES AT HIS POINT OF INTEREST, OR WHERE THE INTEREST OF HIS SUBCONSCIOUS MIND IS FOCUSED, EITHER CONSCIOUSLY OR UNCONSCIOUSLY. TO THE DEGREE IN WHICH HIS INTEREST IS AROUSED, TO THAT DEGREE DOES HIS DETERMINATION BECOME A FACTOR IN LESSENING OR INTENSIFYING HIS DESIRE FOR A REPETITION OF THE EXPERIENCE OR A SIMILAR ONE, AND THIS DETERMINATION AND INTEREST ATTRACT FURTHER EXPERIENCES WHICH DEVELOP EITHER THE CREATIVE OR DESTRUCTIVE SIDE OF HIS NATURE.

EVERY DISCORDANT CONDITION IN THE LIFE OF MAN IS MERELY ENERGY MISDIRECTED, HENCE EXPRESSED DESTRUCTIVELY. Therefore, if an individual is expressing his nature in the wrong way he should

not be opposed but his attention should be directed to some method of expression more interesting than the method to which he has given activity. By this procedure the trouble will at once
be adjusted and removed, while at the same time
constructive expression will be afforded and true
development and unfoldment will naturally result.

OPPOSITION always causes discord. A more
constructive change of attitudes, convictions and
habits of thought, will not only adjust the diffi-
culty but will prevent its return or further manifestation.   A CONSTRUCTIVE ATTITUDE
ALWAYS PRODUCES A CONSTRUCTIVE
RESULT.

Harmony is merely the result of harmony as a
first cause, for the Law works at mental or Spiritual Cause, material effect. Harmony in the mind
must attract harmonious conditions, circumstances and people into your life and if your life
outwardly is indicative of discord, you may know
that your quality of thought is discordant.

YOU MUST HAVE A CONSTRUCTIVE
QUALITY OF THOUGHT, A CLEAR VISION
AND CONTINUITY OF CONSCIOUSNESS IF
YOU WOULD HAVE YOUR LIFE REFLECT
PERFECTION.

VI

Meditation

Its Laws and Uses in Revealing Talent and Ability

MEDITATION IS ALWAYS A THOUGHT PROCESS BY WHICH A QUESTION IS ASKED MENTALLY AND THE ANSWER RECEIVED MENTALLY; HENCE PROJECTIVE AND ATTRACTIVE.

All thought is either attractive, selective or projective; it is selective because it determines what shall be the nature of your creations; it is attractive because it is magnetic; and it is projective because it has intent and reaches from one magnetic center of consciousness to another.

If you consciously direct your thought to another, you immediately make a mental impression upon him which will correspond to your idea, but which will be interpreted by him according to his convictions, attitudes and ideas of you and life in general. However, if he is concentrating upon some idea of his own which he is consciously developing and which is entirely different from your own, then he may not catch your thought, but if he is in a passive mental state, or not consciously directing his mental energy, then your thought will impinge upon his subconscious mind. Perhaps your thought will be held there as an impression until circumstances shall energize it and force it to take outward form.

THOSE WHOSE MENTAL FORCES ARE
SCATTERED, OR ARE NEVER CONSCIOUS-
LY DIRECTED OR CONCENTRATED UPON
CONSTRUCTIVE ACCOMPLISHMENT AL-
WAYS BECOME SERVANTS AND FOLLOW-
ERS OF THOSE WHOSE MINDS ARE DIREC-
TED ACCORDING TO SOME SCIENTIFIC
FORMULA OR ACCOMPLISHMENT.

Those who do not apply the Great Law in be-
half of their own development, are those who are
constantly complaining that circumstances are
ever against them and complain that they are
held back because they lack education, social position and financial standing.

When you become a conscious operator of the
Great Law, not only unseen forces, but those
misdirected, uncontrolled human beings with
whom you are surrounded also do your bidding
and are ever ready to obey your slightest desire.

The most effective method of training the subconscious mind to do your instant bidding is
through meditation and concentration. Meditation focuses its attention and concentration impels it to immediate action, although consumma-
tion may not be realized until conditions and circumstances are so arranged that perfection will
be the natural result of your conscious direction.

Meditation should always precede concentration and should be practiced religiously at regu-
lar intervals in periods of fifteen minutes or
more each. This orderly arrangement and continuity manifest as an orderly arrangement of
manifestations.

The best time for meditation is before arising

in the morning, at noon, before luncheon if possible, just at sundown or shortly after, and before going to sleep at night. Problems of financial and business activity should receive attention during the morning and noon period of meditation, and domestic, social and spiritual matters should be given attention during the sundown and late evening periods.

The science of this system lies in the fact that material vibrations are most active during the early morning hours and until about four o'clock in the afternoon, in your part of the world.

Early morning is also the logical time for meditation because the destructive vibrations are not so intense during this period and the ether is more magnetic with the life forces — all Nature is being revitalized by the sun and there is greater power of attraction for material things because of this fact.

The emotional vibrations are most active from four in the afternoon until midnight. Shortly before sundown and for some time after Nature is storing up vital forces with which to build or sustain herself during the hours of lessened activity, which last from eleven P.M. until about three A.M.

Scientists claim that more souls pass out of the body before midnight and shortly after than during any other period of the twenty-four hours and the reason is that the life forces are less active at this time.

LOVE IS LIFE, AND WHEN THE LOVE VIBRATIONS ARE LESSENED NATURALLY THE LIFE FORCES BECOME LESSENED

ALSO, FOR LIFE IS THE EFFECT OF LOVE.
A DAY WITHOUT LOVE IN THE HEART
AND LIFE IS A DAY WITHOUT GOD, AND
A DAY WITHOUT GOD IS A DAY WITHOUT
LIFE, FOR GOD IS LOVE, AND LOVE IS
LIFE.

Meditation should always take place directly
before going to sleep at night, as the Superconscious Mind should be given control during your
period of rest. This acts not only as a protec-
tion, but many of the most difficult problems are
solved by this mode of meditation.

Nothing but love should fill the thoughts prior
to sleep, love for humanity, and gratitude for the
many blessings and seeming trials of the day, realizing that troubles are but occasions in which
opportunities are hidden. The opportunity is re-
vealed if the attitude is constructive, but remains
hidden if the attitude toward the condition or
circumstance is destructive, because THE ATTI-
TUDE OR QUALITY OF THE THOUGHT AL-
WAYS DETERMINES THE RESULT.

Unlimited success and knowledge belong to
those who can visualize the right conditions and
magnetize their creations with Love, Truth and
Faith. The projection of Love thoughts, sent
forth with conviction and in a scientific way, will
attract Love and Love's manifestations to you.

Best results are obtained when perfect inde-
pendence is adhered to; that is, you should be dependent upon the Universal Consciousness alone,
either for your supply or knowledge, NEVER
UPON INDIVIDUALS OR CONDITIONS, FOR
THESE HAVE ABSOLUTELY NOTHING TO

DO WITH THE CAUSE OF KNOWLEDGE OR
SUPPLY.   THE QUALITY OF YOUR CON-
SCIOUSNESS ALONE IS THE CAUSE OF EV-
ERY CONDITION IN YOUR LIFE.

The wrong dependence of attitude is well il-
lustrated in the case of the woman who killed
herself and three little children because her husband had deserted them and left them without
any visible means of support. She felt absolutely dependent upon HIM for the sustenance of
life, and without HIM she could see nothing a-
head but starvation and misery for herself and
children, because her conscious mind was in control and this mind of limitation limited her supply to only one human source, instead of to her
Infinite Source of All Supply, which is unlimited
and inexhaustible.

MISERY AND SUFFERING ARE IN EX-
ACT PROPORTION TO THE CONTROL OF
THE CONSCIOUS MIND, WHILE PEACE,
PROSPERITY AND HAPPINESS ARE DE-
TERMINED BY THE CONTROL OF THE SU-
PERCONSCIOUS MIND. Rev. George C. Gol-
den refers to the conscious mind as "the desert
land which separates you from your paradise."

Meditation calls into action the subconscious
and the Superconscious minds and holds in
abeyance the conscious mind, or the objective
mind, until the knowledge or wisdom sought is
received. This does not mean passivity in the
least degree, but a positive, receptive mental attitude.

A positive attitude is a listening attitude, with
the attention focused upon some problem to be

solved. When you are listening, you are always in a positive, receptive mental condition and this condition is important if the best results are to be obtained.

By projecting a question into the ether, the important features concerning your question and the relative thoughts and the capacity for your development, is thus flashed across your mental vision.

To clear the consciousness of all thoughts except those pertaining to the subject at hand, allowing them to form or gather to them the thought-findings or impressions concerning your question, is the proper way of meditating. These impressions are sometimes very faint, but if they are constructive, and they will be if the thoughts are magnetized with Love, Truth and Faith, they should be acted upon, no matter how unimportant they may seem to the conscious mind, for the conscious mind always sees limitation and always the natural order of the Law.

You should sit in a listening attitude with your question fixed in your consciousness, just as though you had asked the question of another person and were listening for his answer, and in this way you prevent your subconscious mind from taking any suggestions except those given by your Superconscious Mind. By this process the individual consciousness of the operator is not subject to the destructive vibrations in the surrounding ether, and therefore is not demagnetized by stronger mentalities.

If you have learned the art of concentration and discrimination through previous study and

experience, your periods of meditation will bring
more satisfying results at the start, but on the
other hand, if you have a consuming desire to
gain knowledge and power that you may be of
greater service to humanity, then you will succeed quickly even though you have been a most
destructive thinker.

Your dominant desire to serve humanity will
act as deterrent of the old mental habits by gaining the undivided attention of your subconscious
mind and redirecting it along constructive lines.
I know of no truer promise than, "Ask and ye
shall receive, seek and ye shall find, knock and it
shall be opened unto you." Absolute sincerity in
your seeking, asking and knocking, will determine the result.

Your answers at first may be very faint, but
often these faint impressions, when followed, result in very great constructive changes in the
life and environment of an individual.

YOUR DECISION TO ACT UPON THE AN-
SWERS YOU RECEIVE, AS THE RESULT OF
YOUR MEDITATION, IS A VERY IMPORT-
ANT FACTOR IN GETTING QUICK RESULTS
AND MAKING YOUR LIFE EXTREMELY
INTERESTING.

If you allow your conscious mind to make your
decisions you open the door for doubt and failure,
for the conscious mind always sees limitations
and every imperfection; it deals only with externals and is fearful of everything not within
reach of the physical senses and their reasoning;
as a consequence, you will be continually disap-
pointed; but if you allow only your Supercon-

scious Mind to make your decisions, then all monotony will disappear from your life and your environment will reflect constructive activity.

Where any impression received as a result of meditation inspires you to think, speak or act in a constructive manner, it is to be followed, for such inspiration comes from the Divine Source of All Good. THAT WHICH INSPIRES IS GOOD, OR GOD.

Scientific meditation is the result of four attitudes: first, THE REVERENT ATTITUDE should receive your full attention until you feel the thrill of the spiritual life lifting you above the pettiness of human bickering and discord; the second attitude should be THE QUESTIONING ATTITUDE, which is the predominant quality of meditation; the third essential in meditation is THE LISTENING ATTITUDE, which makes you attune to the Creative Forces in the universe, which are always positive. While you are in this positive condition no destructive vibrations can get control of you and it is thus that you preserve your individuality.

The fourth attitude of perfect meditation is the relaxed or receptive mental condition of the operator. When you are relaxed, but positive, your magnetic quality is of the highest order and you then become a dominant power for the attraction of all good.

You are never indifferent when you have once cultivated the correct attitude of meditation but are mentally alert at all times, recognizing the fact that every person, every circumstance and every condition respond to your power.

It is essential for the new student to spend much time in meditation, for MEDITATION REVEALS TO THE INDIVIDUAL HIS PLACE IN THE UNIVERSAL PLAN AND THE PARTICULAR SERVICE NECESSARY FOR HIS UNFOLDMENT AND SUCCESS. IT REVEALS YOUR VISION IN ALL ITS PURITY AND BEAUTY, AND EACH STEP YOU SHOULD TAKE IN THE PROCESS OF UNFOLDMENT.

REFUSE TO FOLLOW YOUR VISION BECAUSE OF A FALSE SENSE OF DUTY OR INFERIORITY AND ONLY THE DIREST RESULTS WILL FOLLOW YOU.

FOLLOW YOUR VISION BECAUSE THAT IS GOD-GIVEN AND ALL ELSE WILL BE ADJUSTED, BECAUSE OF THE GREATER POWER WHICH YOU HAVE PUT INTO OPERATION BY TAKING YOUR PLACE IN GOD'S PLAN FOR HUMANITY.

By taking your place in life, you will put into operation the Law of Adjustment, which will arrange every condition of your life in accordance with God's plan for your further advancement and afford you the freedom to follow the light of your vision with the fullest cooperation of the Cosmic Forces. Any seeming defeat will be but the transition period from a lesser to a greater opportunity.

MEDITATION DEVELOPS TALENT AS ASSOCIATION DEVELOPS CHARACTER. Meditation creates harmony. Feel the harmony of Life in the silence of the forest; there is no audible music save that of the rippling waterfall or the sweet song of a bird in the branches overhead, yet the vibrations of harmony so fill the soul with intoxication of the fulness of Life that one can only listen in reverence and awe. There, alone, away from the mad rush after selfish happiness, one feels the sacredness of the individual life. Inspired to lofty aims of achievement, one realizes to what unlimited fulness the life can develop if the individuality is kept free from sordid interests.

Meditation creates leadership, because it develops talent and reveals the vision of attainment by connecting you with the Universal Mind so that your thoughts are rays of Divine Wisdom. It is this keeping in tune with the Oversoul or the Universal Source of Knowledge and Power which makes a thinker and vitalizes both the individuality and personality.

It is said that only one person in every twenty-five thousand really thinks, and that not more than one in one thousand ever gives the Superconscious Mind control. Every individual thinker must become a leader because of this fact, and attract the number of people who need his guidance and example of power as an inspiration for their achievement.

Meditation clears away the mental rubbish which the conscious mind has gathered, that the Superconscious Mind, or the Love Consciousness may have control.   OPPORTUNITY EXISTS FOR EVERY HUMAN BEING, AND LEADERSHIP IS FOR EVERYONE WHO WILL APPLY THE GREAT LAW.

"Pray without ceasing," is a Divine Command that means very little to the average person and really seems an impossibility unless the true meaning is discerned. Every good desire for yourself or another is really prayer, and the highest and best quality of prayer there is.

Praise also is prayer if the praise is sincere, for sincerity is a Divine attribute. Gratitude to God and man for any or all blessings constitutes one of the requisites of true prayer. The Bible says, "With praise and thanksgiving let your requests be made known unto God," because those qualities are necessary to true prayer, and prayer is never answered unless it conforms to Divine Law.

The prayerful attitude is the first attitude necessary to meditation, so to feel the proper reverence one must be thrilled with praise to God and thankful for the Omnipotent Power He has bestowed upon the human channels of Divine Wisdom, which are creators with Him.

When you desire good for yourself or another that you may glorify God, your prayer is bound to be answered. "Ye ask and receive not because ye ask amiss that ye may consume it upon your lusts," such is the judgment of God upon the individual who prays for the blessings of life that he may satisfy only his personal pleasures of sense, and not because he wishes to demonstrate to those about him the great and beautiful message of the Creator that "Love is the fulfilling of the law."

Jesus said, "Father, the hour is come; glorify thou me, that I may glorify Thee." Such is true prayer, and the proper attitude to be in when you enter your period of meditation.

If your consciousness is constantly dwelling upon good desires with the determination that your demonstrations may "give hope to mortals crushed by sorrow and terror" and who are also seeking a way out of their "Slough of Despond," then you are complying with Divine Law and YOUR PRAYERS WILL BE ANSWERED, FOR YOU WILL HAVE COMPLIED WITH THE DIVINE COMMAND TO "PRAY WITHOUT CEASING."

Meditation as a valuable aid to demonstration cannot be overestimated, but unless it is done in a scientific manner it becomes a hindrance, rather than a help. "This book of the Law shall not depart out of thy mouth; but thou shalt MEDITATE therein day and night, that thou mayest observe to do according to all that is written therein: for then thou shalt make thy way prosperous, AND THEN SHALT THOU HAVE GOOD SUCCESS."—Joshua 1: 8.

VII

Concentration
Its Laws and Uses

IN OUR study of the sub-conscious mind and its place of power in human destiny, we have learned the value of MEDITATION AND CONCENTRATION in training this great and wonderful servant to do our slightest bidding. There are many methods for training, reaching and directing this faculty of consciousness, but no method is complete unless it incorporates CONCENTRATION as the principal factor.

In demonstrating health, happiness or prosperity, collective or individual needs, there are three activating principles which must receive attention before the desired result can be realized. These three potent factors of perfect demonstration are: DESIRE, DECISION AND CONCENTRATION. No perfect demonstration can be made without them.

There can be no thought process without visualization, hence desire, in its last analysis, becomes a form of concentration, through the making of mental pictures. DESIRE forms the mental matrix or blueprint of what you wish; DECISION focuses the Cosmic Forces; and CONCENTRATION sets these forces in motion and manifests that which you have created mentally. Half-formed or apathetic desire can be intensified and given an added impetus by specific concentration.

My definition for CONCENTRATION IS:

THE FILLING-IN PROCESS OF MENTAL PICTURE MAKING. Concentration by this method becomes very easy and is much more productive of results than the method of holding your attention to a general outline without filling in the details. Begin your period of concentration with a mental outline of the condition or object which you wish manifested in your life, then follow it up to the minutest detail until your picture is complete.

This method clears away everything not relative to the desire and holds the interest and attention of your subconscious mind to the fullest realization which can be attained. After the period of concentration, resultant impressions will come into your mind and these impressions should receive your earnest consideration and be followed whenever they can be developed without undue haste. Always remember that harmony is the important condition of life.

Concentration, contrary to the usual way, should always be practiced with the eyes open; the cones of the eyes being the physical centers used in the projection of thought, the rods of the eyes being the physical mechanism used for the receiving of thoughts. Your scientific application of concentration should make you a great central sending and receiving wireless station for the perfection of any idea which you are trying to develop.

You are a perfect, living, breathing radio station of which your eyes are one of the most important parts. USE YOUR EYES FOR THE SENDING AND RECEIVING OF THOUGHTS

WHICH ARE CONSTRUCTIVE AND EX-
PRESSIVE OF LOVE, TRUTH, FAITH, ETC.,
AND YOU WILL FIND YOUR EYES IM-
PROVING IN STRENGTH, VISION AND
BEAUTY. Eyes that are well-developed and
lustrous, with large pupils, always denote one
who is capable of constructive thinking along in-
tellectual or spiritual lines.

The quality of the consciousness during concentration is as important as the quality of mind
during the period of meditation, because Love,
Truth and Faith must become crystalized into
your creation if you would make it a blessing to
yourself and those who are near and dear to you.

Love opens the door to success, while hate, its
opposite, not only closes the door but locks it and
all efforts to open it will be in vain until the consciousness is changed. Love is the attracting
element and is the activating principle in the
Law of Attraction.

Students who have by previous education and
training or experience, acquired the art of concentration and discrimination will obtain greater
and quicker results in the beginning than will
those whose thought forces have never been con-
served or directed rightly. CONCENTRATION
DIRECTS , CONTROLS, AND CONSERVES
THE COSMIC CONSCIOUSNESS IN ITS IN-
DIVIDUAL EXPRESSION.

The clearness with which you make your mental picture will determine the rapidity with which
the manifestation of your desire will take place.
Unlimited knowledge and success along any line
belong to those who can visualize the right con-

ditions and magnetize their creations with Love, Truth and Faith.

A thought of love should always be followed by LOVING SERVICE. Putting a thought of love into activity, or giving it expression through action, crystalizes it into actual outer form and substance in your life. EXPRESSION GIVES LIFE TO YOUR THOUGHTS AND SENDS THE WAVES OUT INTO THE ETHER TO BE CARRIED INTO ETERNITY, INFLUENCING OTHER MINDS FOR GOOD OR ILL, ACCORDING TO THE QUALITY WITH WHICH THEY WERE SENT FORTH.

TRYING TO DO ANYTHING, LIES IN ACTUALLY DOING IN PART THAT WHICH YOU DESIRE TO DO; HENCE, WHEN YOU DESIRE ANYTHING IN YOUR LIFE OR ENVIRONMENT, YOU WILL DO SOMETHING TOWARD MAKING IT A REALITY. AND IN SPITE OF SEEMING OBSTACLES AND HANDICAPS, THERE IS ALWAYS SOMETHING TO DO RIGHT WHERE YOU ARE THAT WILL FURTHER THE DESIRED MANIFESTATION. THE NEXT STEP TO BE TAKEN IN THE SOLUTION OF YOUR PROBLEM ALWAYS LIES RIGHT WHERE YOU ARE. THE KEY TO THE SITUATION IS ALWAYS WITHIN REACH.

You should have the idea of giving the greatest possible service to those who will be associated with you in sharing the benefits of the manifested desire. This idea should be a subconscious state of mind during the period of concentration, for SUCCESS AND SERVICE ARE SYNONY-

MOUS — YOU CANNOT HAVE ONE WITH-
OUT THE OTHER.

There is always an uneven exchange of benefits whenever you attempt to get the best of a
bargain, which is nothing less than robbery on
your part. To get the best of a bargain without
an attempt to equalize the service is to steal
property belonging to another.

THE DOMINANT CONDITION OF PER-
SONAL LIFE IS ABSOLUTELY INDICATIVE
OF THE DOMINANT THOUGHT CREATIONS
OR MENTAL PICTURES FORMED BY AN
INDIVIDUAL. Take poverty, for instance; this
means a poverty of the love vibrations, for Love
is the Creative Principle of the universe; hence,
the CREATOR OF EVERYTHING WHICH IS
GOOD OR WHICH ADDS TO YOUR HEALTH,
HAPPINESS OR PROSPERITY.

THERE CAN BE NO TRUE CONCENTRA-
TION UPON CONSTRUCTIVE ISSUES WITH-
OUT THE LOVE ELEMENT. Mental pictures
are made from unformed Cosmic Force or Energy and you convert this Energy into concrete
form of like quality as your thoughts.   If the
quality of your own thought corresponds to the
Cosmic vibrations of Love, your picture-making
energy is of the highest order; hence, constructive and magnetic, and your concentration becomes objectified in your life as health, happiness and prosperity.

If you are not expressing Love, Truth, Faith,
Gratitude and Praise, then your picture-making
energy is destructive and becomes objectified in
your life as ill health, poverty, misery and many
other forms of unloveliness.

VIII

Affinities in the World of Ideas

LIKE the grouping of floating magnets, the human magnetic centers of Mind also group themselves according to the quality and intensity of their thought vibrations.

The Cosmic Ether is the Divine Energy or Creative Force without which no life could exist, but in addition to Life Force, it is also Initial Impulse taking various forms through which to manifest ALL of its infinite qualities. Man is only one but the most perfect channel given form, through which to manifest, and when partaking of his Divine inheritance, he becomes a perfect expression of the Divine qualities. Because of this, man was placed a step higher than the animals and given the power to use his mind as he sees fit. In fact the Bible states that man is "little lower than the angels," and this is a fact, for we are "created in the image and likeness of God" and are co-creators with Him.

The animal is guided by instinct but man is given the power to think and to form the kind of thought pictures he desires; also to control and direct them as fancy dictates. With this power, he forms mind-pictures by his desires, and by concentration and meditation he directs the Divine Energy which creates and manifests whatever it receives directions for creating. The Cosmic Energy is for the manifestation of all good and is inhaled and exhaled automatically and rhythmically with every breath.

The thought emanations of man, which have been projected into the ether for ages, are inhaled and exhaled with every breath, according to the control and direction of the individual consciousness. Man can control this human picture atmosphere, or "mortal mind" as it is called by some metaphysicians, or he can be controlled by it.

The God Consciousness is the larger inheritance of mankind and the mortal consciousness is the lesser inheritance, both to be used constructively and according to Divine Law, which is Psychological Law. All knowledge is abstract until by attraction and expression it becomes concrete. All knowledge is common property and is for the benefit of all peoples.

Because each individual was created to attract and express, not only some one quality as his dominant vibration, but all the qualities of Divine Mind, every mentality acts upon every other mentality and lesser forms of consciousness, influencing those of like quality and directing and controlling the weaker ones. This is the reason why man, through his direction and control of Divine Energy, can and does control all created manifestaitons of Nature except the individual expression of humanity.

Man was created for the education of himself and for the service and education of other members of the race. By reason of this fact, all thought-pictures formed by the mind of man are created by man's use of Divine Energy and are made manifest, therefore, by projecting a thought you always attract an effect relative to the individual life.

If we wish success in any line of endeavor, it is important that we train our minds to become receptive to the highest and best vibrations of the HUMAN thought atmosphere, as well as to the Divine Consciousness. The automatic electricity of Divine Energy is a carrier into the human consciousness of the mental germs of the thought atmosphere which the Cosmic Consciousness causes to bud and blossom into fragrant flowers of Mind. Professor Elmer Gates, of Washington, D. C., who is eminent in chemistry, electricity, biology, and psychology, makes the statement that "Through the power of Mind, inventors can be made to order and discovery promoted. Genius has been an accident hitherto; in the future, it will be created systematically."

Your opportunity is always, because being a magnetic center of Mind, your good fortune flows to you as a river flows to the sea, providing of course, that you work according to Law and Order. No matter where you are, if your mental state is vibrant with Love and its many attributes, you become the center of money, love, and power.

Like the electricity used for light, whenever a heating or power device is attached to the individual channel, the volume of light is lessened. So it is with the motive power of thought; whenever it is used for destructive purposes, the power for constructive work is depleted.

If, by some quality of thought, you have attracted to yourself some disagreeable condition or unbearable relationship, it will be useless to run away from it or rail against it as an unkind Fate. You will be enslaved by it, or similar conditions and relationships, until the quality of thought which attracted them is entirely eliminated from your consciousness, or modified to a marked degree. If a condition or person has been attracted to you by a thought of hate or intense selfishness and you ignorantly intensify the condition by hating the more, you may be driven to crime or suicide unless the love vibrations are brought to bear upon the situation.

Each human or animal affinity or related condition, mirrors alike our faults or our virtues according as we love or dislike them, or express the same faults or virtues ourselves. This is why a practitioner can only heal by increasing the faith and knowledge of his patient by presenting the Truth to his subconscious mind, either through MENTAL OR VERBAL SUGGESTIONS; AND IT IS THE ACCEPTANCE OF THE TRUTH, BY THE SUBCONSCIOUS MIND, WHICH DOES THE WORK. IT IS THE INHERENT POWER WITHIN WHICH PERFORMS THE MANY SEEMING MIRACLES ATTRIBUTED TO THE HEALER.

To hold resentment in the heart because of past injustice is a tremendous factor in the ability to fail. You cannot grasp the grand possibilities of the future until you let go of the PAST with its false conceptions and destructive memories. To drag the rotting fabric of the past into the healthy tapestry of the present is to contaminate the whole and lessen its durability for

future use. You should never be concerned about
what others have done or will do to harm you,
for if there are no wrong or unjust thoughts in
your own heart, no one will injure you or yours,
for the perfection in your own life will bring a
corresponding quality of understanding and love
into the lives of your dear ones, raising their individual vibrations to such a quality that they
will be supplied and protected to a greater degree than ever before. The result will be determined by your understanding and application
of Universal Law. Be very sure there is no injustice in your own thoughts and then you will
not judge or condemn others.

At each mile-post the burden of the past should
be cast aside and the journey onward be resumed
with new zeal, fresh energy and greater hope.
Thus the goal is reached with all the vigor of
youth unimpaired and the crown of merit gained
with nothing from the past to dim its glory.

Each day some portion of the debris, within
the temple of the soul, should be cleared away,
until at last can be seen that which Reality has
proven does not belong to a far-off land where
golden sunshine and azure skies were possessions
to be acquired, but to the present where all good
awaits the earnest seeker after Truth and knowledge.

The sun is always shining where you stand.
The Kingdom of the Sun is within, but the win-
dows are darkened with the accumulated filth
that has been allowed to find entrance and lodge-
ment on the sacred mirror of the soul. We are
centers created for the manifestation of love,

and the building is from within.   The outward
conditions should reflect the Divine Nature, but
this depends entirely upon the individual work-
man.   Close application to the Law and a striving
for perfect execution will bring the golden reward.

IX

Faith, Hope, Charity

FAITH, hope and charity; these three qualities of Mind, are three of the fundamentals of all successful psychological phenomena dealing with individual life problems. When analyzed and applied, they become dynamic factors in demonstration but one without the other is an instrument neither efficient nor complete.

There are two kinds of Faith, blind and intelligent; but the blind faith is the poorest substitute in the world for the real quality of Mind. Every thinker has intelligent faith, while any number of people who follow where the thinker leads, have only blind faith. The rest of the people have little or no faith at all, and become the human parasites of the race. BLIND FAITH IS IGNORANCE; INTELLIGENT FAITH IS UNDERSTANDING OF UNIVERSAL LAW. MAN SHOULD BE EDUCATED INTO HIS CREED OR FAITH, NOT BY IT; AND THIS EDUCATION SHOULD BE THE RESULT OF INVESTIGATIVE THOUGHT ON HIS PART. WHEN FAITH IS ACQUIRED IN THIS MANNER, IT BECOMES UNDERSTANDING. AND IF FAITH IS UNDERSTANDING, THEN IT MUST BE SUBSTANCE, FOR IT IS THE PRACTICAL WORKING HYPOTHESIS BY WHICH IS CREATED THE STRUCTURE OF SUCCESS.

Those who are willing to be led let the thinker

solve all the issues of life and simply take his word that all is as it should be or as he sees it. The unthinking mind seems to feel that it is less effort to let the leader do the investigating; but this shirking of duty is dearly paid for in misery and suffering. Thought, unless controlled and directed properly, is a destructive force that consumes more energy and time than any human being can afford to lose.

HOPE IS DESIRE. But desire without faith is impotent; hence, faith is the substance of desire or hope. Desire forms a mental picture which Faith and Love cause to become manifest in the material world. Faith then, is the evidence of things not seen by any save the individual director and the Universal Consciousness. WHERE THERE IS FAITH, THERE IS NO DOUBT OR WORRY FOR BOTH QUALITIES ARE DUE TO A LACK OF FAITH. This means faith in man as well as faith in God; for to doubt man is to doubt God. Each individual is a creation which God has caused to become manifest for a special purpose; and to doubt the very channels through which God manifests is to close the door to our own good. OUR FAITH IN GOD, THEREFORE, IS IN EXACT PROPORTION TO OUR FAITH IN MAN.

The fundamental principle of charity is love. Charity, from time immemorial, has meant to the unthinking that quality of giving which always tends toward pauperization, and as a consequence, real charity has suffered from disuse.

In love there is no pauperization; only a wish to pass along or share the manifestations of Life and Love, and a little of the kindliness which contributes so much to happiness and hastens the coming of Universal Brotherhood. CHARITY THAT PAUPERIZES IS ALWAYS PROMPTED FROM A DESIRE TO DISCHARGE ONE'S OBLIGATIONS OR A DESIRE FOR APPROBATION FROM ACQUAINTANCES AND FRIENDS. THIS SORT OF CHARITY IS CRUELTY AND SNOBBISHNESS. REAL CHARITY IS LOVE AND SINCERE FRIENDSHIP, AND ANYTHING WHATSOEVER GIVEN WITH THE TRUE SPIRIT NOT ONLY INSPIRES THE RECIPIENT OF THE GIFT TO A BETTER ATTAINMENT, BUT RAISES THE DONOR TO A HIGHER PLANE OF THOUGHT AND SERVICE.

TO DEVELOP OUR NATURES WE MUST GIVE; TO ACCOMPLISH INTELLIGENTLY WE MUST GIVE; FOR ALL LIFE IN ITS PERFECT EXPRESSION IS A SCIENTIFIC MANIFESTATION OF THE LAW OF EXPANSION AND ATTRACTION, OR GIVING AND RECEIVING. Life becomes disorganized on any other basis of operation. All harmony is the result of this law put into effect. Every cause must have a related effect or result; hence the more you give, the more you will receive, but whatever is received will be of like quality with the thought which prompted the initial gift.

Mental cause and effect might be likened to respiration, because for everything you give, in word, thought or deed, you receive something in return. Every thought which you project into the ether brings back to you some possession or

condition. IF YOU GIVE SCIENTIFICALLY
YOUR GENEROSITY WILL NEVER MAKE
YOU POOR, NOR WILL IT PAUPERIZE
THOSE WHO ARE FAVORED BY YOUR
LOVE.

The instant you begin to hoard what comes to
you, or keep it for yourself alone, a congestion
takes place in the Cosmic Ether around you and
becomes manifest in your life as discord.   TO
GIVE WITHOUT LETTING GO IN MIND
PRODUCES   THE   SAME   RESULT   AS
THOUGH YOU HAD NOT GIVEN AT ALL,
FOR IT IS THE THOUGHT ACTION WHICH
OPERATES. The Mind is the Heart of the Universe and there MUST BE CONTINUOUS, AU-
TOMATIC, SCIENTIFIC ACTIVITY IF DIS-
ORDER WOULD BE PREVENTED.   All Nature evolves by Law and Order, automatically
and rhythmically; it is a constant flowing of
everything pertaining to Life and whatever in-
terferes with the Life current causes inharmony.

When the continuous, automatic flow of breath
is interfered with, ill health and death results,
and so it is with the Law of Giving and Receiving;
to receive and refuse to give, or give only to
those you love very dearly, causes the death of
the soul and prevents its Divine unfoldment. For
every selfish thought there is a corresponding
detrimental result.

No pauperization can take place if you give
according to Nature's law: gladly, freely and lovingly. Love, like the sunshine, does not promote
a luxuriant growth unless it is abundant and
free. You should share with those less fortunate,

projecting good thoughts with every gift, for the
two go together. Mind is the chemist in the lab-
oratory of Life, and Love is the chemical which
potentizes all conditions of destructive fer-
mentation. Possessions which come to us as the
result of love and the projection of love thoughts
are never lost through force. We must vibrate
only the conditions we wish manifested. To visualize evil pictures, even with the honest desire
to eliminate the evil condition, is but to intensify
it in some other form. To fight evil is like giving
a crude drug instead of a potentized remedy; it
never cures the cause but merely relieves the surface manifestation of the disease, forcing it to
appear in worse and more intensified condition
through another channel.

IT IS NOT WHAT YOU SELL TO THE
WORLD, BUT WHAT YOU GIVE TO THE
WORLD, THAT BUILDS YOUR LASTING
SUCCESS. Whatever you sell should carry with
it the very best of your effort; to sell an inferior
article, or that which will not benefit, or for an
exorbitant price, is a boomerang that will act dis-
astrously upon yourself. Abraham Lincoln attained to the presidency of the United States,
but was it the money he made during his term
of office that has made him a figure in history
which will live? No! It was what HE GAVE
TO THE WORLD which makes his name re-
vered by all. However, we can give scientifically
and so reap prosperity as well as homage.

In giving, you should never try to impress the
individual or group of people with the importance
of your gift, nor the greatness of its value. It

should be given, not as a bounty of YOUR GEN-
EROSITY, but rather as a gift it is your PLEAS-
URE to bestow.   Also, you should never ask nor
bargain for a return favor, or an even exchange.
Your gift should be the result of an inward impulse to express love, and if given in this way
the value and importance will be fully apprecia-
ted and an even exchange must follow; perhaps
not in the coin you expect but in something which
you need.

No one can express true love until it is felt
within the secret recesses of the soul.   Thoughts
constantly vibrating Love must feel an impulse
for outward expression and this is why an expression of sincere friendship is always recognized as such.   The most ignorant human being,
and even the creatures of the animal kingdom,
as well as the lower forms of consciousness, can
sense it.   Sincerity is ALWAYS sensed and there
MUST be a response.

This same law applies to all that expresses evil.
The Creative Force or Initial Impulse is always
of the same quality; the difference lies in its use
and application; the desire determines how it
shall be expressed. This explains how one having
a great capacity for evil has as great capacity
for good.   The capacity, once created by the desires, remains to be filled with good or evil con-
tents.

To accept more than we give, without the desire to render loving service in return, is to create an uneven balance which must be finally adjusted by us, and this fact is usually the cause
of so many disagreeable changes in life.   A per-

fect balance is gained by giving more than we receive, for by so doing a capacity for receiving more is created, and this capacity must be filled. When you cease to receive good it is due to the fact that you are not giving scientifically, or are creating evil conditions by thinking wrongly. We receive only in proportion to the quality of our giving or serving.

It is the receptive attitude of Mind that attracts knowledge and understanding. This does not engender a sense of superiority or rulership, but rather a greater sense of loving service.

X

Cellular Consciousness and the Psychology of Food

"For he that eateth and drinketh unworthily, eateth and drinketh damnation to himself, not discerning the Lord's body. For this cause many are weak and sickly among you, and many sleep." 1st. Cor. 11: 29-30.

"If any of them that believe not bid you to a feast, and ye be disposed to go; whatsoever is set before you, eat, asking no question for consciousness sake. For if I by grace be a partaker, why am I evil spoken of for that for which I give thanks? Whether therefore ye eat or drink, or whatsoever ye do, do all to the glory of God." 1st. Cor. 10: 27-30-31.

IN PREVIOUS chapters you have been taught how each discordant, destructive thought brings forth manifestations after its kind. You were also taught how the expression of any destructive emotion, such as hate, fear, anger, envy, unkind criticism, etc., produces poisons in the system which must manifest in the body as disease; intensity and quality determining the intensity and quality of the manifestation. Mental and spiritual harmony produces harmony of body and environment, which mean health and happiness.

The basis of every manifestation of disease is mental or spiritual discord, and the basis of health and happiness is mental and spiritual harmony.

While medical doctors can discover and name the kind of germ which accompanies and is typical of certain diseases, they fail utterly in defining *the cause which produced the disease and the germ.* They find certain germs in a locality which is very unprepossessing or in a home where the conditions are such as to make ALL implications of uncleanliness absolutely false and so the cause of the disease is attributed to impure water or food. However, people all over the country are dying of the same diseases, yet who are not drinking the same water or eating the same kind of food, and the attending physicians are blaming the conditions to nearly as great a variety of things as there are victims. And this in spite of the fact that it has been demonstrated time and time again that no matter whether the disease was diagnosed as the result of bad water, food or environment, THE RIGHT MENTAL ATTITUDE CAN AT ONCE SO CHANGE THE CHEMICALIZATION OF THE BODY AS TO MAKE ALL TRACES OF THE DISEASE DISAPPEAR INSTANTANEOUSLY.

Medical men also have a fine faculty for NAMING every discordant condition of the body and pronouncing HOPELESS those cases which they fail to relieve. THEY FAIL TO FIND PAIN AND CAN ONLY RELIEVE IT BY ADMINISTERING DRUGS, WHICH PARALYZE THE MENTAL FACULTIES AND OFTEN CAUSE THE PATIENT TO ACQUIRE HABITS WHICH DESTROY THE SOUL. Thus the medical means of alleviating pain is sometimes worse than the disease, for at best, the relief is but temporary and the effects of the means used often does more damage than the ravages of the disease itself. In spite of all this, doctors have their place in the world and often do a splendid work among those who are not ready to accept anything more than is offered them through the channels of medical practice.   Even in Metaphysics, recognition is made of the beneficence of an anaesthetic during great suffering or when a surgical operation is being performed.

HOWEVER, A SURE RELIEF FROM PAIN IS WITHIN THE REACH OF EVERY SUFFERER, AND THE RELIEF FROM TROUBLE AND DISCORD IN THE LIFE IS JUST AS SURE AS THE RELIEF FROM PAIN, BUT IN ORDER TO FIND THIS RELIEF CERTAIN LAWS AND RULES OF CONDUCT MUST BE LEARNED AND APPLIED.

Every discordant condition in the life of man is merely misdirected energy. Being misdirected, it must manifest as discord. A more constructive change in attitudes and convictions WILL AT ONCE ADJUST THE DISTURBANCE AND PREVENT ITS RETURN. A CONSTRUCTIVE ATTITUDE ALWAYS PRODUCES A CONSTRUCTIVE RESULT. HARMONY IS MERELY THE RESULT OF HARMONY AS A FIRST CAUSE.

THE QUALITY OF THE THOUGHT SENT FORTH, AS WELL AS THE INTENSITY OF THE INITIAL IMPULSE, AT THE TIME OF PROJECTION, ALWAYS DETERMINES THE RESULT. VIOLENT ATTITUDES OF HATE, ANGER, JEALOUSY AND UNKIND CRITICISM ALWAYS PRODUCE VIOLENT RESULTS IN THE LIFE.

Each attitude and conviction is creative according to its kind. As an example, let us take anger. If your anger is intense and your motive is physical injury, you will attract bodily injury to yourself; if your anger is intense and you desire disturbing conditions in the life of another, then these same conditions will come into your life, because what we wish for another we create for ourselves. If, on the other hand, your anger is expressed in unkind criticism, you intensify the fault which engendered your criticism, thus bringing it into your own life, where it will be expressed by those of your own immediate family, husband, wife, children, etc.

SO IT IS THAT ALL PHASES OF HATE, ANGER AND UNKIND CRITICISM PRODUCE RHEUMATISM, SICK HEADACHE, NEURALGIA AND LUMBAGO, BECAUSE THE LAW OF LIFE IS ABSOLUTE AND THOUGHT CREATES AFTER ITS KIND.

Stomach trouble is also caused by unkind criticism; in fact, ALL PAIN IS CAUSED BY JUST THREE STATES OF CONSCIOUSNESS — HATE, ANGER AND UNKIND CRITICISM, FOR PAIN IS PURELY MENTAL VIBRATION ACTING OR REACTING UPON THE CONSCIOUS MIND AS PAIN. IN OTHER WORDS, PAIN IS A VIBRATION OF HATE, ANGER OR UNKIND CRITICISM IN THE SUBCONSCIOUS MIND, BEING TRANSMITTED TO THE CONSCIOUS MIND AS PAIN. ELIMINATE ALL HATE, ANGER AND UNKIND CRITICISM FROM YOUR HEART AND YOU WILL NEVER FEEL ANOTHER PANG OF PAIN, EVEN THOUGH YOUR BODY BE TORN TO PIECES.

These three qualities of hate, anger and un-
kind criticism steal upon one unawares, imping-
ing upon his subconscious mind and robbing him
of his royal birthright of leadership. Should you
complain if the Law of Compensation or Divine
Justice metes out to you the exact consequences
of your thievery and malicious hatred? THOSE
WHO ARE SURROUNDED BY THOUGHTS
OF HATE, EITHER IN THE FORM OF AT-
TRACTED OR PROJECTED VIBRATIONS
ARE ALWAYS FULL OF FEAR.   FEAR,
THEN, IS ALWAYS AN INDICATION OF
HATE. "WHERE THERE IS LOVE, THERE
IS NO FEAR, FOR PERFECT LOVE CAST-
ETH OUT ALL FEAR."

The next phase of disease which will be brought
to your attention is the manifestation of physical
impurity — catarrh, boils, abscesses, colds in the
head, scrofula, running sores, infection and all
forms of pus conditions. EVERY MANIFES-
TATION OF THIS KIND FINDS ITS CAUSE
IN AN IMPURE MENTAL STATE.

THE FOREGOING STATEMENT MEANS
JUST ONE OF THREE THINGS: EITHER
THE PERSON SUFFERING FROM ONE OF
THESE FORMS OF DISEASE IS CREATING
THE DISTURBANCE THROUGH A DOMI-
NANT IMPURE MENTAL CONDITION, OR
BECAUSE HE IS ALLOWING HIS MIND TO
DWELL UPON THE IMPURITY OF OTHERS,
OR ELSE HIS MIND IS DWELLING UPON
THAT PARTICULAR MANIFESTATION OF
DISEASE; AND WHATSOEVER THE MIND
DWELLS UPON MUST BECOME MANIFEST

IN THE LIFE IN SOME CONDITION OF
GOOD OR EVIL, ACCORDING TO THE QUAL-
ITY OF THE THOUGHT.

You ask, "How does this theory account for
an infant suffering pain and disease?" And I
say to you that a child is but a sensitive instru-
ment or center of Consciousness WHICH REG-
ISTERS THE THOUGHTS OF THE ADULT
MENTALITIES WITH WHICH IT IS SUR-
ROUNDED, PARTICULARLY THE MENTAL
ATTITUDES AND CONVICTIONS OF THE
MOTHER.

Until a child is fourteen years of age, HIS
PHYSICAL CONDITION IS LARGELY THE
RESULT AND REFLECTION OF THE IM-
PRESSIONS AND SUGGESTIONS IMPLANT-
ED BY THE ADULT MINDS WITH WHICH
HE IS CONSTANTLY ASSOCIATED. Many
of these suggestions have been prenatal and it is
the prenatal suggestions of the mother which
build the body of the unborn child and determine
its physical condition at birth and until it is
fourteen years of age, sometimes longer, according to whether the mother is a woman who
dominates those about her or whether she is
sensible, loving and intellectually and spiritually
developed.

There have been many instances of nursing
babies having been killed by the poisoned milk
of the mother because of her destructive mental
condition. All so-called infant's diseases are the
manifestations of parental thinking, and by eliminating or changing the disease-producing
thoughts of the parents, you cure the disease of

the child. IT IS MOST IMPORTANT FOR THE PROSPECTIVE MOTHER TO KEEP HER THOUGHTS PURE AND SWEET, NOT ONLY DURING PREGNANCY, BUT DURING EVERY MINUTE THAT SHE HAS THE CARE AND TRAINING OF HER CHILD TO CONSIDER.

ALL congestion in the body is caused by chronic opposition. Heart trouble is the specific result of such mental opposition, and you never saw anyone who was greatly distressed by this disease who did not have that trait developed to a high degree. They are invariably those who constantly oppose personal liberty for others and who constantly dictate to those about them, only content when they are bending others to their will. Sometimes this opposition is confined to the relatives and intimate friends of the family, but it is just as insidious in its effects even though it may not be noticed by those outside of the family circle; it may only exist between husband and wife or between parents and children, but nevertheless, it is deadly in its effects upon every department of life.

JEALOUSY, ENVY, GREED, AND UNKIND CRITICISM, CAUSE LIVER TROUBLE AND BILIOUS ATTACKS. Constipation is caused by opposition. Fear and feverish mental conditions cause fevers. Fear for the health of a child may and does produce fevers that are common to child life. From fourteen years until twenty-one the dominant mental and spiritual attitudes of parents and relatives become manifest in the life of a child as habits, conditions, inherited tenden cies, and these influences act as obstacles or aids in the financial, domestic and social life of an individual after he is twenty-one, acting as reactions upon any new suggestions which may be received or upon opinions which he may form as the result of independent investigation.

Often times, one's conclusions and opinions are formed because of parental suggestions and these suggestions are aired as one's personal views. Opinions thus formed are always ignorant and are recognized as such by others, who attribute them to hatreds and prejudices. Such a display of opinions ignorantly formed belittles one in the eyes of others and prevents human association which would benefit all parties concerned, for ASSOCIATION DEVELOPS CHARACTER AS MEDITATION DEVELOPS TALENT.

Hatred and prejudice, in whatever form, are always the result of ignorance, which is a lack of personal investigation, and always dwarfs the individual growth and hinders individual achievement. If you wish to succeed in a big way, refuse to accept the opinions and convictions of your parents or your friends as your own until you have investigated all sides of the issue for yourself and proven its worth. YOU CANNOT MAKE ANY FURTHER PROGRESS THAN HAVE YOUR PARENTS AND FRIENDS UNLESS YOU THINK DIFFERENTLY THAN THEY. YOU MUST INVESTIGATE FURTHER ALONG THE SAME ISSUES AND ALSO ACCEPT NEW IDEAS AND LINES OF THOUGHT.   YOU CANNOT MOVE IN THE SAME GROOVE THEY HAVE MADE AND

MAKE A PLACE FOR YOURSELF. YOU MUST MAKE A PLACE OF DISTINCTION FOR YOURSELF BY EXPRESSING YOUR OWN TALENTS AND EMOTIONS IN YOUR OWN WAY, LETTING ONLY "THE VOICE OF THE SILENCE" BE YOUR GUIDE.

Anger is the cause of erysipelas, apoplexy, high blood pressure and painful accidents, scalds, burns, broken bones and sprains. ALL VIO-LENCE IN THE LIFE IS CAUSED BY VIO-LENT EMOTIONS AND THE VISUALIZA-TION OF VIOLENCE. Cancer is the result of smothered hate, envy and unkind criticism, and can never be permanently cured by drugs nor op-erations, unless one's current of thought is also changed. "DISEASE CANNOT BE CUT OUT, ONLY THE MANIFESTATION CAN BE CUT AWAY."

OPERATIONS SOMETIMES RELIEVE THE SUFFERER FOR A TIME, BUT CANCER CAN BE CURED BY MENTAL MEANS.

Irritations of the skin are caused by mental ir-ritations, and the more acute the mental disturb-ance, the more acute will be the physical mani-festation. Various kinds of itch, rash, eczema, etc., come under this classification. Paralysis is caused by fear, different kinds of fears causing different forms of the disease.

There is no reason why a human being should die after the manifestation of a disease takes place, for that is really the time one should begin to recover, providing, of course, that nature re-ceives co-operation in her efforts to throw out the accumulated poison. This co-operation should

be in the form of NATURAL REMEDIES SUCH
AS HAVE BEEN PROVIDED BY NATURE
FOR THAT PURPOSE.   THE MANIFESTA-
TION OF A DISEASE IS THE RESULT OF A
VOLUME OF ACCUMULATED POISON THAT
THE NATURAL FUNCTIONS OF THE BODY
HAVE FAILED TO ELIMINATE IN THE
NORMAL WAY. This accumulated poison must
be thrown off and is forced out of the system in
an unnatural way.

The accumulated poison would cause death if
it were not purged from the system quickly; so
you see, that a manifestation of disease is not
only an indication that the blood is being purified,
but that the manifestation is acting as a "safety
first" means of restoring one to normal health.
IT IS THE FEAR OF DISEASE WHICH IS
AROUSED MENTALLY THAT ADDS TO ITS
ALREADY ABNORMAL AMOUNT OF POI-
SON AND MAKES IT IMPOSSIBLE FOR THE
BODY TO EXPEL IT; THIS, AND THIS
ALONE, causes death. However, the chemical-
ization of the body can be CHANGED AND
REGULATED ABSOLUTELY BY MENTAL
MEANS, AND GOOD, WHOLESOME, NOUR-
ISHING FOOD.

Eliminate any destructive mental quality and
YOU WILL FIND THAT YOU HAVE PER-
MANENTLY CURED YOUR BODY OF SOME
PHYSICAL DISCORD.

To prove that your mental state determines
even your appetite and the kind of food that your
body requires, change your mental attitude and
convictions and you will find that your desire for

food has changed to correspond to your new state of consciousness.

When you desire certain kinds of food, it is because your mental attitudes have created certain demands for the chemicals that are most necessary for the proper activity of making the body reflect the state of consciousness which you possess at that time.

NO OTHER FOOD THAN THE FOOD YOU DESIRE WILL PROPERLY NOURISH YOUR BODY UNTIL YOUR MENTAL QUALITIES HAVE CHANGED, BUT ON THE OTHER HAND, THE FOOD YOU HAVE FORMERLY DESIRED WILL NO LONGER NOURISH YOUR BODY AFTER YOUR MENTAL HABITS HAVE BEEN SUBLIMATED. A WELL-BALANCED PERSON WILL PARTAKE OF AND ENJOY ALL NOURISHING FOOD, ALTHOUGH HE MAY HAVE AN UNPREJUDICED PREFERENCE FOR SOME CERTAIN KINDS. THERE SHOULD BE NO HATRED FOR ANY KIND OF FOOD, FOR HATRED OF WHATEVER SORT RESULTS IN PHYSICAL DISCORD. IF YOU ANALYZE THIS STATEMENT AND DECIDE TO EAT ALL FOODS, YOU WILL FIND IT VERY EASY TO ACQUIRE THE HABIT WHICH CORRESPONDS TO YOUR DECISION.

Eating food because you think you ought to eat that particular kind of food will never produce the desired result, for dieting never produces permanent results because of this truth. If your mental processes create a demand for food which contains iron in order that your body may respond to a certain state of consciousness, it will be useless for you to eat food containing an abundance of lime and eliminate the food containing iron. While one element can never take the place of another, yet the blood must contain all the elements and chemicals, fourteen in number, which are needed to keep the body normal but the exact proportion is determined, or should be determined, by the subconscious mind and the quality of consciousness.

For instance, if one is ill as the result of anger vibrations which have filled the blood with poison, the first thing necessary is to change the quality of mind, then use simple, natural means to eliminate the accumulated poison, following which, eat the foods to correspond with the changed state of consciousness, or what the subconscious mind creates an appetite for.

The effort of each individual should be to acquire a normal, or well-balanced consciousness by developing the entire man, physical, mental and spiritual, and then eating a well-balanced diet, that the subconscious mind may have all the material at hand to use in building the body according to the mental condition.

In order to have the body reflect a well-balanced mind, fourteen chemicals are required to be in the blood at all times, and these chemicals, or blood and nerve salts, are carried into the body by the food you eat, the water which you drink, and the air you breathe, fresh air and pure water being very essential in the maintenance of perfect health. WATER SHOULD BE FRESH, NOT BOILED, FOR BOILING CHANGES THE

NATURAL OR CHEMICAL COMPOSITION, AND MANY OF THE NECESSARY ELEMENTS ARE ENTIRELY LOST BY THIS PROCESS.

PHOSPHORUS is absolutely essential to the perfect chemicalization of the blood, for without PHOSPHORUS there is no sparkle to the eye, no vim to the actions and little or no elasticity to the muscles.   The foods that best supply this chemical in the greatest degree are the electrical foods, so called, given here in the numerical order of their chemical value: lemon, pineapple, grapefruit and orange.

These fruits often seem to cause an eruption of the skin and serious disturbances of the stomach and bowels.   This disturbance is due, either to the fear of the condition, sometimes prenatal, or to the action of the fruit chemicals upon poisons which have been previously deposited in the blood by destructive moods.   The natural electrifying of the blood by a constructive change of consciousness and the electric foods, forces these accumulated poisons out of the system and it is this activity which causes the disturbance.

EVERY INDIVIDUAL CONSTANTLY DISPLAYS TO OTHERS THE DOMINANT CHARACTERISTICS OF HIS TYPE, IN VOICE, FACIAL EXPRESSION, CARRIAGE, AND HABITS OF EATING, DRINKING, SLEEPING; IN FACT, EVERY GESTURE OF AN INDIVIDUAL INDICATES AND REVEALS THE MAN WITHIN, OR THE SUBCONSCIOUS ACTIVITY.

Those who eat almost exclusively of sweets,

pie, cake, cookies, ice-cream, candy, French pastry, etc., and who care little for any other kind of food, are those who have not learned the true value of really worth-while things and are undeveloped mentally; those who touch life only on the surface.   The thoughts of these people are not the strong, deep, creative thoughts of vital issues.   One does not seek such people for encouragement, comfort or inspiration.   The love of such an one is a very elemental emotion and fails to satisfy; instead, it very often repels the object of its emotion, until a separation takes place.

So it is with other types; the savage man or woman requires savage food, plenty of meat, with potatoes and bread and coffee, by way of variety; he requires the most elemental food in order that his face and form may reflect his state of mental development.   By savage, I mean those with an accentuated dictatorial attitude.   Those who devote their time and energy in driving others to do their bidding and who have their way at the expense of another's comfort, just for the mere satisfaction of having their way.

A well-balanced person likes all kinds of food and enjoys what he eats.   DISLIKING OR HATING DIFFERENT KINDS OF FOOD IS BUT ONE WAY OF EXPRESSING THE SUBCONSCIOUS QUALITY OF HATE, AND FOR THIS REASON, IF FOR NO OTHER, ONE SHOULD LIKE ALL GOOD, NOURISHING FOOD.   If one partakes of a well-balanced diet at every meal, the body is constantly supplied with an abundance of every chemical necessary for the perfect action of the subconscious mind, and it then has at hand its choice of those chemicals needed for perfect reflection and functioning at all times.

Each cell of your body is like a drop of dew, a tiny mirror which reflects the state of consciousness which creates it.

EVERY THOUGHT IS TRANSMITTED TO EACH CELL BY THE ACTION OF THE SYMPATHETIC NERVOUS SYSTEM, AND EVERY MENTAL PICTURE WHICH YOU HOLD IS THE ACTIVATING ENERGY WHICH IMPELS YOUR SUBCONSCIOUS MIND TO ACTION, FOLLOWED BY INSTANT RESPONSE FROM EVERY CELL. THE CELLS RESPOND INSTANTANEOUSLY AND AUTOMATICALLY TO WHATEVER MENTAL SUGGESTION IS GIVEN THE SUBCONSCIOUS MIND AND THIS IS WHAT IS CALLED CELLULAR CONSCIOUSNESS.   THE ENERGY WHICH IMPELS YOUR SUBCONSCIOUS MIND TO ACTION IS CALLED PICTURE-MAKING ENERGY.

You can readily see that you are only treating effects when you diet in order to change your physical condition, and that it is absolutely necessary for you to change your mental attitude and pictures and then the question of proper food will be adjusted more correctly than by following rules of diet and exercise first.

Another important factor in preventing and eliminating disease, or accumulated poisons in the system, is the care of cooking utensils and dishes. ANY DISH IN WHICH FOOD IS COOKED OR PREPARED SHOULD BE SCRUPULOUSLY CLEAN — "CLEANLINESS

IS GODLINESS AND ORDER IS HEAVEN'S FIRST LAW."

The mentality which neglects this important item is a mentality devoid of personal pride, consideration of others, self-respect; in other words, such a person is selfish, shiftless, careless, thoughtless and without true culture — consequently such attitudes react destructively upon the system, which becomes disorganized and filled with physical impurity, for the body always reflects the quality of consciousness. Cleanliness and orderliness thus become an aid to perfect health, because a clean, orderly mentality creates a clean, orderly body.

THE END